THE NOVELS
OF
FRANK NORRIS

THE NOVELS
OF
FRANK NORRIS

by

Donald Pizer

INDIANA UNIVERSITY PRESS

Bloomington & London

For June

PREFACE

Critics have approached Frank Norris and his work in various ways. He has been psychoanalyzed by Maxwell Geismar and Kenneth S. Lynn, studied as a disciple of Zola by Marius Biencourt and Lars Ahnebrink, and placed in the context of American naturalism by Ernest Marchand and Charles C. Walcutt. Franklin Walker has written his biography and edited his letters, and numerous scholars have contributed articles on special aspects of his work and on particular novels. But despite this abundant interest in Norris, there has been no attempt to interpret fully the nature and quality of each of his novels.

There have been two major obstacles to such an endeavor. The first is the tradition of Norris as a "natural," as a writer who, in his own words, used "his heart, his senses, his emotions, every faculty but that of the intellect." Norris did indeed pose as an anti-intellectual, and many of his ideas and themes derive from his primitivistic core of values. But anti-intellectualism and primitivism are themselves intellectual constructs, and Norris' novels are philosophical novels in the sense that they contain coherent systems of belief and value. We are not deterred from examining Wordsworth's ideas because he believed that impulses from vernal woods were more profound than the learning of sages, and we should not be deterred in Norris' case either. The second major hindrance to a full and clear reading of Norris' fiction has been the almost inevitable tendency to begin all discussions of his work with an examination of his naturalism. Too often Norris' work has been interpreted and evaluated in relation to an abstract philosophy of naturalism to which he never subscribed. He has frequently been victimized by the inclination of critics, as noted by James T. Farrell, "to create a category of naturalism, and then to use the category as a means of judgment." Norris' central values are neither derived from nor similar to Zola's, and any interpretation of his fiction which begins with a search for Zolaesque ideas is bound to conclude that Norris was a muddled thinker whose novels are undeserving of intensive study except, perhaps, to prove how muddled he was.

I therefore will not discuss Norris as the "boy Zola"—that is, either as unthinking "natural" or as confused disciple. Nor will I take up cohesively or fully his biography, his short stories and criticism, his literary borrowings, or the general literary and social scene of his time. Rather, I will explore Norris' mind and art primarily by discussing his ideas and his novels, with particular emphasis on *Vandover and the Brute*, *McTeague*, and *The Octopus*, referring to other aspects of his work, career, and times as they shed light on his novels. For if Norris has any claim to lasting interest, it is as a novelist and particularly as the author of these three novels.

My thesis is that Norris' novels are all of a piece—that when he writes of nature as machine in *Vandover*, or of McTeague's better and brute self, or of Bennett's iron will, or of Force in *The Octopus*—that all of these arise out of a coherent conception of man, nature, and God, though they derive from different parts of that conception. In my first chapter I will take up the sources, nature, and implications of this system of ideas; in later chapters I will discuss each of his novels both in relation to this system and as a fictional entity. In short, this book is in part an exercise in history-of-ideas criticism. I hope to show how a writer absorbed a particular contemporary system of belief, how he modified and adapted this belief in accordance with his temperament and background, and how he transformed it into fictional theme, symbol, and form—into a McTeague or a Moran, into an Arctic adventure or the growth of a crop of wheat. From another angle, this book is a study in how the imagination creates the material of fiction out of the interaction between the issues of an age and the personal experience and temperament which are brought to bear upon those issues.

I will try to avoid implying that to explain Norris' system of ideas, both as a whole and as it appears in each novel, is to find that Norris was a successful philosophical novelist. Explication will serve as a means toward judgment rather than as the equivalent of judgment. A plot incident may symbolize a particular theme and yet be poorly imagined and constructed. But it is, perhaps, not too simpleminded at this moment in the history of the criticism of fiction to reassert that a full awareness of a novelist's central values is a necessary prelude to critical evaluation of his work.

D.P.

ACKNOWLEDGMENTS

I have profited greatly from the Frank Norris and Franklin D. Walker collections at the Bancroft Library, University of California, Berkeley. The first was assembled largely through the efforts of Professor James D. Hart, the second—consisting primarily of invaluable notes for Norris' biography—was donated by Professor Walker. Mr. Frank C. Preston, Jr., has kindly granted me permission to quote from unpublished Norris material, and Professor Walker to use his notes. The staff of the Howard-Tilton Memorial Library, Tulane University, has met my excessive demands with generosity and understanding. I am indebted to the following individuals for their aid and comment in connection with this book: Joseph M. Backus, Robert Brownell, Stanley Cooperman, William B. Dillingham, Margaret Groben, James D. Hart, F. W. J. Hemmings, Franklin Walker, and Charles C. Walcutt. I owe much to the careful reading of my manuscript by Richard P. Adams, E. P. Bollier, and Marvin Morillo. I have drawn frequently on much of the published commentary on Norris, and also upon several excellent unpublished dissertations. I try to indicate these debts in the notes and bibliography. Portions of this book, in different form, have appeared in *American Literature, American Quarterly, PMLA,* and *Texas Studies in Literature and Language.* I wish to thank the editors of these journals for permission to reprint.

ACKNOWLEDGMENTS

This book was written during a year's leave of absence made possible by the John Simon Guggenheim Memorial Foundation and the Tulane University Council on Research.

CONTENTS

THE NOVELS
OF
FRANK NORRIS

Chapter One

INTRODUCTION

The central themes of Norris' novels are closely related to the foremost intellectual dilemma of his time: the conflict between traditional concepts of God, man, and nature and a growing body of scientific knowledge impinging on those concepts. In the decades following the publication of *The Origin of Species* many Christians who no longer required a literal interpretation of the Bible were nevertheless troubled by the Darwinian hypothesis. Although they were willing to sacrifice Genesis, they were not willing to relinquish God the purposeful designer of man and the universe. The Darwinian principle of random variation, however, left little room for teleology; it presented a history of life dominated by chaos and chance. Moreover, the Christian conception of human history and future as Paradise, Fall, and Redemption through supernatural Grace seemed incompatible with the Darwinian view of that history and future as a continuous specialization of function through natural process. Lastly, nature was no longer God's second self, guiding and addressing man—as nineteenth-century romantics in particular had come to think of it—but was rather the principal agent in the struggle for existence, indifferently destroying those incapable of adapting to its conditions.

A primary mode of resolving this conflict was to substitute

a more malleable evolutionary theory for Darwinism—that is, to think of evolution in some other way than natural selection alone (strictly speaking, Darwinism is the theory of natural selection) and thereby put to rest some of the disturbing ideas raised by the implications of evolution.[1] It was above all Herbert Spencer who offered such a substitution. Spencer's usefulness to Christian evolutionists derived from several characteristics of his synthetic philosophy, as he called his system. First, unlike Darwin, he was a cosmic theoretician. Evolution was at the center of his philosophy, but his primary endeavor was to explain and categorize all existence, somewhat as a formal theologian might. Moreover, he did not limit evolution to natural selection but rather considered natural selection among other factors causing evolutionary progress. Lastly, though Spencer was an agnostic who relegated first causes to an Unknowable, he denied that he was a materialist, leaving the way open for a theistic adaptation of his system.

This adaptation was particularly feasible because Spencer's synthetic philosophy rested on the law of the conservation of energy, a law more amenable to theistic interpretation than that of natural selection. He argued that the basic constituent of the universe was force, though this force or energy took the correlated forms of matter, motion, space, and time. Evolution, to Spencer, was a universal process of change from incoherent homogeneity (the unspecialized and simple) to coherent heterogeneity (the specialized and complex) caused by the omnipresence and persistence of force. The adaption of living things to their environments was but one part of this process of change. Spencer's world, like Darwin's, was dynamic and unified (man and nature inseparably linked in a process of change), but it differed from Darwin's in that it was a world of ordered, not chaotic, dynamicism. Spencer had shifted the idea of order from that of static

4

similarity to that of interrelated change, but he had preserved the idea. In short, unlike Darwin, who tried to divorce his findings about species from cosmic evolutionary laws and from ideas of progress, Spencer found that universal natural laws were leading men to perfection and happiness. And the step from a beneficent natural law to God's providence on earth is a very short one for anyone theistically inclined.

Spencer's ethical scheme was also capable of a religious interpretation, though his ethical ideas offered more problems to theists than his cosmology. Spencer's ethics combined the two great streams of nineteenth-century ethical theory. On the one hand, he posited a Darwinistic utilitarianism (later called Social Darwinism) in which the struggle for existence within natural selection was morally justifiable because it had brought the greatest good to the greatest number: the emergence and development of the human race. On the other hand, he believed that individual moral choice was intuitively utilitarian, that the racial experience of man had produced an inherited moral sense (Spencer was a Lamarckian) which was fundamentally utilitarian. Spencer could thus argue that man instinctively chose what was best for the race or group, a position capable of translation into the orthodox idea that man possessed a God-given intuitive moral sense, which instructed him to think of others before he thought of himself. However, some disturbing ideas were present here for Christian evolutionists, since this instinctive striving for the racially best might involve a struggle with others in which only the fittest survived.

Finally, Spencer was more palatable than Darwin because he offered the possibility of confirming, within a "modern" philosophy, popular faith in free will and in progress. The law of evolution, as stated by Spencer, operated independently of man in a cosmic determinism. Spencer, however, did not deny free will to individual man, for he believed that each man molded his own fate by freely choosing his degree of harmony with his material and social world. Some men might succeed more than others, but the total movement of mankind was toward greater and greater adaptation and ultimate perfection.

It is not surprising, then, that most English and American evolutionary theists—such men as Lyman Abbott, Henry Ward Beecher, Henry Drummond, and John Fiske—tended to bypass Darwin for Spencer. Although all these clergymen and writers were popular and influential, I shall concentrate on Fiske as the best example of an evolutionary theist, since his beliefs most resemble the generic reconciliation of religion and science accepted by many Americans of the time, including Norris.

Fiske, an acknowledged disciple of Spencer, attempted to return God to Spencer's synthetic philosophy. Fiske held that basic religious faiths—for example, those of God as purposeful designer, man as center of the universe and possessor of an immortal soul, and the reality of free will and moral justice—were expressed by natural law. Man had to go *Through Nature to God*, Fiske declared in the title of one of his books, rather than try to find Him in formal theology or the Bible, though the truths which Fiske found in nature's laws were not very different from traditional Christian belief. Of course, there were some discrepancies between evolutionary theism and conventional Christianity, particularly as regards Christ and salvation. In general, however, Christian evolutionists like Fiske felt that they not only had rescued religion from the threat of science, but had used science to confirm the great traditional religious truths.

Fiske found God in nature by declaring that Spencer's omnipresent, indestructible force was God. To Fiske, therefore, God was immanent in all nature and in nature's processes and laws, though God also existed independently of nature. All is God, but God is not all, Fiske argued. All phenomena are intelligible "only

6

when regarded as the multiform manifestation of an omnipresent Energy that is in some way—albeit in a way quite above our finite comprehension—anthropomorphic or quasi-personal."[2] Evolution, therefore, is a process both designed by and embodying a "quasi-personal" God. It is, above all, His means of achieving the development of the human soul and the priority of soul over material life. God is not so much the watchmaker to Fiske; He is rather *in* the emergent flower, directing from within the growth of that which most resembles His own essence—man's spirit.

Spencer had not clearly distinguished between "psychical" force (mind or soul) and material force (all outside mind or soul). Evolutionary theists such as Fiske, however, tended toward a strict dualism, since they held that the human soul was the greatest product of evolution and was that which distinguished man from other living things. This dualism was immediately available as a means of dealing optimistically with the problem of evil. Evil was the persistence in man of certain animal instincts which had had a role in man's development but which were now obsolescent. The progress of evolution, Fiske wrote, is toward the "perfecting of man . . . mainly in the ever-increasing predominance of the life of soul over the life of the body" as "the ape and the tiger" die within us.[3] "Original sin," Fiske summed up, is "neither more nor less than the brute inheritance which every man carries with him, and the process of evolution is an advance toward true salvation."[4] The importance of Fiske's reworking of Christian ideas into evolutionary terms is not only that this reworking reaffirms the tendency toward dualism within Christianity and uses this dualism to help explain the problem of evil. His belief is also important because it translates supernatural ideas about the fall and salvation of man into concrete human qualities in man's past, present, and future, and thus makes these ideas capable of symbolic representation in realistic fiction.

Evolutionary theists used much the same method of transmuting the supernatural into the natural when they approached one of the central cruxes in any ethical interpretation of evolution: if man had advanced to the possession of a soul through evolution, why did he still participate in a ruthless struggle for existence? Christian evolutionists solved this problem by conceiving of God as a kind of modified utilitarian, a role required of Him if the evident hardships and sufferings present in the struggle for existence were to be reconciled with a faith in a God both immanent and benevolent. Adapting Spencer's utilitarianism, Fiske argued that although individuals might experience pain and destruction in the struggle for existence, the species, race, or society benefited from the presence of these evils. The implication was that God selected and was immanent in a process which provided for the greatest good for the greatest number. Evil was therefore an inevitable but negligible and transient factor if one kept in mind the large cosmic movement toward good. Moreover, man—because of the increasing role played by spirit—was advancing toward a mode of social progress based on cooperation rather than warfare. Fiske believed that although strife was still a current method of progress, "a stage of civilization will be reached in which human sympathy shall be all in all, and the spirit of Christ shall reign supreme throughout the length and breadth of the earth."[5] Fiske, therefore, answered Huxley's famous Romanes lecture, in which Huxley argued that it was impossible to reconcile Christian ethics and the law of the survival of the fittest, in two ways—that natural selection was no longer the only or even the dominant mode of social evolution, and that natural selection had helped produce what Huxley was calling for, a rule of Christian love. Nature may appear cruel, Fiske wrote, but

> profoundly underlying the surface entanglements of her actions we may discern the omnipresent ethical trend. The moral sentiments, the moral law, devotion to unselfish ends, nobility of

soul,–these are Nature's most highly wrought products, latest
in coming to maturity. . . . Below the surface din and clashing
of the struggle for life we hear the undertone of the deep ethical
purpose, as it rolls in solemn music through the ages. . . .[6]

There is one more theistic adaptation of Spencer by Fiske which
is important. If Spencer's force is God, nature must not only be
benevolent, its laws eternal and omnipotent, but these qualities
of Godhead must also be perceivable by man—man must be able
to intuit knowledge of God by experiencing nature. In other
words, the idea of immanence is closely allied to that of transcendentalism. Evolutionary theists such as Fiske thus found the
idea of immanence a particularly attractive way of combining the
older American transcendentalism with the newer evolutionary
faith, for immanence suggested the possibility of an intuitive perception of the divine knowledge present in nature.[7]

Starting from the idea of force as immanence, Fiske translated
Spencer's synthetic philosophy into an acceptable theology rang-
ing from a God-centered cosmology to man's ability to know his
God. He had achieved Henry Drummond's goal for the correct
relationship between science and religion—that "as the Supernatural becomes slowly Natural, will also the Natural become
slowly Supernatural, until in the impersonal authority of Law
men everywhere will recognize the Authority of God."[8] Or, in the
simpler and more immediate lines of a popular poem of the day,
"Some call it Evolution,/And others call it God."[9]

2

Norris encountered a particular version of the late nineteenth-
century reconciliation of science and religion at the University of
California, where he was a student from 1890 to 1894. As an
adolescent he had wanted to be a painter and was much interested

9

in medieval subjects, but by the time he entered Berkeley, at twenty, he had decided to become a writer. His earliest literary work, before he entered California and during his first two years there, consists almost entirely of Kiplingesque short stories (I will discuss these briefly later) and of poems and stories with medieval settings. The latter are particularly interesting, for they contain two elements which were to reappear again and again in Norris' work—sensationalism and moralism. His story "Le Jongleur de Taillebois" (Dec. 25, 1891)* is an excellent example of this combination.

The story opens in the New Forest, where Amelot has just bloodily murdered a man whose body he hides under a tree. Fifteen years later, while lost in the Forest, Amelot is maimed by the same tree when it is struck by lightning. The tree continues to haunt him until at last he is hung from a gallows made of its wood. Like Hawthorne, Norris unites sensationalism and moralism in a dominant supernatural symbol—here the tree and its various guises. The theme of the story is not simply that "crime will out" but that there is a moral order in nature which abhors evil and punishes the wrongdoer. This same combination of moralism and sensationalism appears in Norris' poem *Yvernelle* (written 1889-1890), in which a knight guilty of lust undergoes a tortuous repentance and expiation.

In short, Norris accepted basic Christian ideas about body, soul, and moral order, though at this point in his career he was probably more absorbed in the excitement and detail of his medieval material than in moral and religious problems. He had had ample opportunity to receive traditional moral ideas. His mother was a high-church Episcopalian and a Browning enthusiast, while his father had been a follower of the evangelist Dwight Moody.

---

* Dates in the text are dates of publication. For complete publication information, see the Bibliography.

Moreover, Mrs. Norris, a former actress, read aloud to her children each night from such stalwart moralists as Scott and Dickens.

Norris' lack of intellectual involvement in his early literary work characterized most of his academic career at Berkeley. He was seldom an active student, and he particularly disliked his major subject, English, with its prescribed themes and its analytical approach to literature. Seemingly, too, he took little part in student intellectual life. Yet it would have been almost impossible for him to avoid some knowledge of the primary intellectual concern of students of that day—the doctrine of evolution—just as a contemporary American student could scarcely help having some ideas or opinions about the racial question or the cold war. At Berkeley during the early 1890's, as Franklin Walker has noted, "the enthusiasm for evolution was at its height,"[10] so much so that the historian of the class of 1895 could seriously write: "Evolution! Major spell that opens the gate which bars the single path to all solutions! Philosopher's stone of thought, thou transmutest all base conceptions to the pure gold of Truth."[11] In Norris' freshman year a very active Evolution Club was formed "for the purpose of studying the doctrine of evolution in its various bearings,"[12] and in his junior year its place was taken by a Society for the Study of Ethics and Religion.[13] Evolution was "strong" among students at California, one of Norris' classmates later recalled.[14]

It was also strong among the faculty. Of Norris' teachers, Bernard Moses in history and political science had been trained at Heidelberg and had absorbed the Germanic method of studying social and political institutions in terms of their evolutionary growth.[15] Charles Mills Gayley, head of the English department, had also studied in Germany. Norris took his course in literary criticism, half of which was devoted to the study of "The Evolution of Literature, and the Differentiation of Literary Species."[16]

Discussion and use of evolutionary ideas were all around Norris, then, and whatever his interest in football, class rushes, or fraternities, he could hardly escape some awareness of the principal cause of intellectual excitement on the small Berkeley campus of that time. He encountered evolutionary ideas, however, not only in the inevitable fraternity bull sessions or in the commitment of his teachers in the humanities to some kind of evolutionary hypothesis, but much more directly from Professor Joseph Le Conte, whose courses in geology and zoology he took during his third year at Berkeley.[17] Since Norris' central themes are closely related to Le Conte's thinking about evolution and religion, it is necessary to take up Le Conte's ideas in some detail.

3

Norris' one academic enthusiasm at Berkeley, according to many of his classmates and relatives, was for the lectures of Professor Le Conte.[18] Five times a week throughout his junior year of 1892-93 he attended the lectures of a man who was the most popular professor on campus, who spoke with great force and dramatic effect, and whose twofold object in his teaching and writing was to point out that evolution was not a materialistic theory and that there was no conflict between evolution and traditional religious and humanistic belief. Le Conte felt that it was his duty "to lift science to a recognition of her own glorious mission, that of verifying and at that same time giving rational form to all our noblest beliefs and aspirations."[19]

Le Conte's popularity and his influence on Norris are understandable when it is realized that his courses in geology and zology were quite different from those a student of today might take. The classes consisted of large lecture groups of over a hundred students (there was very little laboratory work) who were drawn to the course primarily by Le Conte's vivid presentation of the dramatic and ethical possibilities of his subject.[20] Both the appeal of Le Conte the man and the attractiveness of his ideas to young minds of his day can be gauged from the following tribute to him in an 1891 student publication:

> The teaching of our Professor of Natural History is character-
> ized by its peculiar charm, a charm which all feel and acknowl-
> edge. As interpreted by him, science appears to have a loftier
> mission than is commonly attributed to it. It is seen in its rela-
> tions to philosophy, to ethics and to poetry; and thus the facts
> which it records are invested with a deeper meaning. There is
> something beautiful and touching in this reconciliation of sci-
> ence and poetry, in this endowment of the natural world with
> the charm which hovers over the world of mystery and fiction.
> From his love of the variety and order and harmony of Nature;
> from his devotion to truth and the loftiness of his ideals; from
> his hearty sympathy with the activities and aspirations of men,
> and his serene faith in the final triumph of good over evil,—there
> comes to us each day an inspiration. We may not express this
> in words; we may give no outward sign of its reception; yet we
> leave the lecture-room with a feeling that we have been in the
> presence of something high and worthy. And these impressions
> are lasting; they are seed from which future harvests are to
> spring.[21]

Le Conte expressed this "reconciliation of science and poetry" not only in his classroom but in his many articles and in his major philosophical work, *Evolution: Its Nature, Its Evidences, and Its Relation to Religious Thought* (1888; 2nd revised edition, 1891). Support for assuming that Norris heard in class Le Conte's pub-lished ideas is found in Le Conte's statement that "Nearly every-thing I ever wrote was first given in my class-room and afterward written out and perfected" and in his famous remark on his role as a popularizer of evolution, "Woe is me, if I preach not the Gospel."[22]

Early in the 1870's Le Conte had been encouraged by Henry Ward Beecher to attempt a reconciliation between religion and the new evolutionary science.[23] In this attempt he was influenced primarily by Spencer and Fiske, though his philosophy was eventually eclectic, embodying ideas of Darwin, Lamarck, and others. Like Fiske, Le Conte carefully distinguished between pantheism and immanence. He rested his evolutionary theism on the premise that "God may be conceived as self-sundering his Energy and setting over against himself a part as Nature."[24] To Le Conte, therefore,

> God is immanent, resident in Nature. Nature is the house of many mansions in which he ever dwells. The forces of Nature are different forms of his energy acting directly at all times and in all places. The laws of nature are the modes of operation of the omnipresent Divine energy, invariable because he is perfect. The objects of Nature are objectified, externalized—materialized states of Divine consciousness, or Divine thoughts objectified by the Divine will.[25]

All nature to Le Conte is thus natural—that is, available to scientific observation and describable by scientific laws—and supernatural, for "all is permeated with the immediate Divine presence."[26]

God has a dynamic rather than a static presence in nature, however, and the process of differentiation of His energy into ever higher and more complex forms is the process of evolution. At a particular point in this process of differentiation, psychic force— or spirit—evolved out of the anima or consciousness of animals and acquired the property of immortality—that is, became the human soul.

One of the primary characteristics of Le Conte's belief was his idea of evolutionary stages—that rather than there being one universal cause of differentiation, specific differentiating factors were dominant at particular stages of evolution. In premammalian life, for example, Lamarckian factors of use and disuse were dominant; in mammalian evolution natural selection predominated. In man, there is a new dominant factor—the human spirit—which for the first time directs evolution not by law from without but by choice from within through the conscious striving of man, guided by reason, toward a spiritual ideal. Each advancing stage, however, incorporated rather than discarded the earlier factors of evolutionary progress. Le Conte wished it to be clear that "although the distinctive human factor is indeed dominant, yet it is underlaid and conditioned by all the lower factors; that these lower factors are still necessary as the agents used by reason."[27] Man still participates in organic evolution—"on this new and higher plane, all the factors of organic evolution must continue to operate as before; . . . as before the struggle for life and the survival of the fittest must operate to perfect the race."[28]

But despite the continuing necessary presence of these "lower factors," Le Conte viewed "the whole evolution of the cosmos through infinite time" as "the gestative process for the birth of spirit."[29] Thus man "alone is possessed of two natures—a lower, in common with animals, and a higher, peculiar to himself. The whole mission and life-work of man is the progressive and finally the complete dominance, both in the individual and in the race, of the higher over the lower. The whole meaning of sin is in the humiliating bondage of the higher to the lower."[30] This ethical dualism is not aceticism, however, for

> True virtue consists, not in the extirpation of the lower, but in
> its subjection to the higher. The stronger the lower is, the bet
> ter, *if only* it be held in subjection. For the higher is nourished
> and strengthened by its connection with the more robust lower,
> and the lower is purified, refined, and glorified by its connection
> with the diviner higher, and by this mutual action the whole

plane of being is elevated. It is only by action and reaction of all parts of our complex nature that true virtue is attained.[31]

Like Fiske, therefore, Le Conte embodied in his evolutionary theism not only various contemporary evolutionary ideas, but also traditional beliefs in free will and in the primacy of spirit over body. Both he and Fiske stressed immanence as the key to the evolution of man's soul and to the reconciliation of natural selection and God's benevolence. He differed from Fiske primarily in that his idea of evolutionary stages gives more permanent roles to natural selection and to man's animal nature while continuing to emphasize the priority of cooperation and spirit.

4

Le Conte's ideas had an immediate and lasting effect on Norris.[32] Why they did, however, is not easily answerable, for Norris did not reveal his deepest nature in letters or in conversation, but only in his fiction. "Frank had few mental friends," Gelett Burgess recalled. "He did his thinking alone."[33] But from what is known of Norris' personal life, and from what can be deduced from his writings, he evidently found in Le Conte two basic ideas which satisfied needs deep within his own temperament. First, he found a confirmation of the belief that there is a moral order inherent in nature and its laws—a belief present in his earliest writings. Second, he found a way of dealing coherently with two aspects of man's animal nature—his sensual drives and his pleasure in violence and conquest—which he felt strongly within his own nature. Le Conte, in other words, supplied Norris not with any new insights, but rather with a way of shaping and confirming his deepest feelings about man and about himself. Howells remarked of Norris that he had "his instincts mostly so well intellectualized,"[34] and it was Le Conte's ideas in particular which Norris seized upon for that intellectualization. Norris was fascinated by the animal drives and the violence which he felt were at the heart of "the black, unsearched penetralia of the soul of man,"[35] yet he was also anxious to affirm certain beliefs about man's free will and spirit. Such a mind, seeking some way of giving unity and form to these feelings, could easily neglect those aspects of Le Conte's evolutionary theism that might trouble a professional philosopher: the leap from Energy to God, for example; or the idea of both a personal and an immanent God; or the suggestion of a streak of cruelty in a God who operates through a law of natural selection; or the indescribable transition from animal consciousness to human soul.

Norris, like many others of his time, sidestepped these and other problems of the philosophy for its two broad central themes—that God is present throughout life as a vast force for good, whatever the harshness of some natural laws, driving on through these laws toward the perfection of the race and a higher spiritual life; and that at present man is of body and soul, with the body the result of man's evolution from animal life and the spirit or soul the distinguishing characteristic of man's evolution beyond animal life. Le Conte's conception of the twofold potential of the animal in man particularly attracted Norris, since these two ways of viewing man's "lower" nature were closely related to Norris' early absorption in warfare and struggle and to his recognition of his tendencies toward gambling, laziness, and sexual adventure.[36] Within Le Conte's system, that part of the animal in man which caused him to strive for conquest was not to be denied. It still supplied the strength and energy necessary if man was to survive in the struggle for existence permeating all life. But those parts of the animal which clashed with the spiritual—that is, sensual pleasure and gross sexual desire—were vestiges of man's animal past hindering his gradual evolution toward the dominance of spirit over body. "Civilization is far from that time when the fighting man can be dispensed with," Norris wrote in 1897, defending class rushes at Berkeley. "The life of men in the world is one big 'rush' after all, where only the fittest survive and the weakest go to the wall."[37] This defense fuses in one image of beneficial struggle Le Conte's idea of the still necessary role of man's "more robust" animal nature; the late nineteenth-century mystiques of the strenuous life and the Anglo-Saxon warrior; and the youthful Norris, whose great project while an art student was an immense canvas of the battle of Crécy—all of these here come together. In the same article on class rushes, Norris went on to compare organized fighting and college dissipation. He concluded that "This fighting business is better than drinking, and cigarettes, and women," revealing his basic moral temper, a temper conditioned by a strong sense of guilt about bodily pleasures and weaknesses. When he expressed this temper in fiction, however, he usually did so within the rhetoric and symbolism of sensuality as an atavistic bestial characteristic, and his metaphors are those of the cave and the wolf.

The immediate impact of Le Conte's ideas on Norris is visible in the story "Lauth," which appeared in the *Overland Monthly* in March, 1893, when Norris was attending Le Conte's courses. The story, set in medieval Paris during a rebellion, is divided into two parts. The thematic relationship between the two parts is not entirely clear unless Le Conte's evolutionary ethical dualism is kept in mind. In the opening part, Lauth, a young scholar, becomes involved in a battle and kills a man. "At the sight of blood shed by his own hands all the animal savagery latent in every human being awoke within him," and in an instant he returned "to the level of his savage Celtic ancestors."[38] Norris was always to delight in sensationally depicting this aspect of man's nature. But the second half of the story in a sense refutes a major implication of the first—that man is *all* animal once the trappings of civilization are discarded and the inner man reveals itself. Lauth is killed, and several of his friends engage in an experiment to revive him, an experiment which reveals the primacy of the soul within man's nature despite the continuing reality and strength of his animal past.

One of the experimenters is Chavannes, a materialist, who argues that death cannot be real, "for life was a force, and force was inexhaustible."[39] Life, he decides, must therefore remain somehow in the body and be capable of restoration. Anselm, on the other hand, is an idealist who believes that the soul is the "motor of existence" and that once it has departed life is forever lost. At first the experiment appears to be successful. Lauth regains consciousness and the ability to speak. But he is abstracted, feels something is lacking, and finally crying *"This is not I,"* falls into a rapid mental and physical dissolution. He regresses to a "dull, brutish torpor," then to an animal-like state, "quite stripped, grovelling on all fours in one corner of the room, making a low, monotonous growling sound, his teeth rattling and snapping together." At last, just before death, "it lived, but lived not as do the animals or the trees, but as the protozoa, the jelly-fish, and those strange lowest forms of existence wherein the line between vegetable and animal cannot be drawn."[40] Lacking a human spirit, Lauth has retrogressed from the highest form of prehuman life to a mass of protoplasm. Anselm now realizes that both he and Chavannes were wrong.

> "You said and believed that life alone was the energy of existence, I, the soul; I think now that it is both. Life can not exist without the soul, any more than the soul, at least upon this earth, can exist without life. Body, soul, and life, three in one; this is a trinity. . . .
> "That which we call man is half animal, half God, a being

19

on one hand capable of rising to the sublimest heights of intellectual grandeur, equal almost to his Maker; on the other hand, sinking at times to the last level of ignominy and moral degradation."[41]

"Lauth" is characteristic of what was always to attract Norris in Le Conte's ideas and of his method of portraying those ideas, despite the difference between this story and Norris' novels. For here are the preoccupations with life as a force and with man's ethical dualism which were to appear in Norris' novels from *Vandover* to *The Pit*. Here, too, is his tendency to naturalize the supernatural—that is, to demonstrate as real within nature and natural law certain religious ideas, a method which leads to Norris' characteristic combinations of sensationalism and moralism and of atavistic and religious imagery.

Thus the transition from the sensational moralism of "Le Jongleur" to that of "Lauth" involves primarily Norris' discovery of a satisfying natural explanation and a fresh dramatic context for his basic sentiments. He had begun in "Lauth" to think about God, man, and nature, but he had not really changed his ideas about them. The advantages of this discovery are particularly clear in his presentation of the theme of immortality. In "Crepusculum" (April, 1892) Norris had stated that "Death's visage wan/Is lighted not with twilight but with dawn."[42] For this shopworn image of rebirth he was later to substitute the fresh and exciting idea of evolutionary theism that immortality is in reality the persistence of energy or force. So in "The Guest of Honor" (August, 1902), death is real, but the greater reality, allowing Norris a new and animated rhetoric, is that of life as "the symphony of energy, the vast orchestration of force, the paean of an indestructible life, coeval with the centuries, renascent, ordained, eternal."[43]

There remains the need to discuss briefly Norris' changing emphasis within his preoccupation with these two aspects of Le Conte's evolutionary theism—nature as an indestructible force embodying God, and the dual nature of man. Throughout Norris' work nature is an immense force moving independently of man in "vast grooves" toward "appointed goals," and he often symbolizes it as a machine. Nature as machine can either destroy or benefit individual man, but it always—being God Himself—ultimately benefits mankind as a whole. Norris does not vary in his image of nature as a vast engine but rather in his choice of what aspect of nature's power to present in interrelation with man's ethical duality. In *Vandover* and *McTeague* he dramatized the fall of men who succumb to bestiality, as natural laws destroy those men who have not kept pace with evolutionary progress, who are handicapped in the struggle for existence by their atavistic bestiality. In his "middle trilogy" of popular novels—*Moran of the Lady Letty, Blix,* and *A Man's Woman*—he went on to develop a theme implicit in *Vandover* and *McTeague,* the ability of man to exploit for good his dual nature rather than be a victim of it— to use brute force, with the aid of "a man's woman," to invigorate moral strength and strength of purpose. In his incomplete trilogy of the wheat, and particularly in *The Octopus,* he described man's ability to perceive the cosmic processes and laws of nature and thereby ally himself with them and fully discover and obey God.

To Norris, nature's indestructible energy is uncontrollable by man, whether that force be expressed in the struggle for existence, in the life cycle of birth, death, and rebirth, or in the law of supply and demand. Man, however, has free will in his individual relationship to force. He can ally himself with it, attempting to perceive its workings and to determine its pace and direction, or he can stand opposed to it and be destroyed. Almost all of Norris' central themes lie within this concept. His work changes primarily from his early interest in the tragic or sensational possibilitics of man destroyed when thwarting nature to his later concern with the ability of man to perceive God in nature and to adjust his life in accord with that perception.

Nature, to Norris, is above all moral. It removes those individuals harmful to the race; it aids those who abide by its rules; and it benefits the race as a whole. Norris reaffirms the ideals of free will and of moral order, but he does so by means of an ethical scheme which finds these values in natural law rather than in revelation. Norris makes nature not only theoretically God, by means of the idea of immanence, but functionally so: within his novels nature is omnipotent yet allows free will; it rewards and punishes; and it is cosmically beneficent.

Norris' total work bears on the age-old paradox of free will and determinism, and he attempts to exploit both the tragic and the hopeful potentials of that paradox. And just as the problem or paradox is old, so Norris' solution is traditional. He accepts the idea that evolution is omnipotent, omnipresent, and benevolent as a process, yet argues that the individual determines his fate by his relation to the process, much as the Christian determines his fate by his relation to God and His laws. Indeed, the natural laws which concern Norris are in essence naturalized versions of conventional Christian belief. Norris occasionally deals with a "sport" who lacks this opportunity to choose, but for the most part his world view embodies a traditional paradox which he attempts to "reword" within the formulas of belief of his time.

Chapter Two

Vandover and the Brute
AND McTeague

1

Much of the planning and writing of *Vandover and the Brute* and *McTeague* occurred at Harvard, where Norris spent the academic year 1894-95. Perhaps he had heard that Harvard, unlike California, encouraged original work in its writing courses.[1] Or perhaps he was drawn to Cambridge by the idea of a year away from the distractions of San Francisco in a situation which would require constant literary production. In any case, he noted in his application for admission that he wished to study at Harvard "to be thoroughly prepared for a literary profession,"[2] and with this end in mind he devoted himself primarily to the writing course given by Lewis E. Gates.

By the time Norris entered Harvard he had encountered almost all the major writers and ideas which were to influence his work. In his freshman and sophomore years at California he had suffered attacks (to use his own imagery) of Kipling and Richard Harding Davis.[3] As a junior he had taken Le Conte's courses, and in his junior and senior years he became absorbed in Zola and read a great number of his novels.[4] Add to this his admiration for Stevenson, Maupassant, and Flaubert—all pre-Harvard enthusi-

23

asms—and one has a literary apprenticeship which hardly seems to proceed in a direct line toward *Vandover* and *McTeague*. Moreover, none of the dozen or so short stories which Norris wrote during his Berkeley years suggests the mode of the two novels which immediately followed them.

The "explosion" of *Vandover* and *McTeague* out of these disparate influences and non-Zolaesque stories can be accounted for in various ways. First, throughout his career Norris considered the short story a minor literary form, to be pursued with neither the intensity nor the integrity required of the novel. The difference, then, between such a slight, imitative story of early 1894 as "Travis Hallett's Half-Back" and the novels Norris began some six months later is not the result of some abrupt change on Norris' part. It is caused by Norris' casual approach to the short story and his serious-minded attitude toward the novel. Even when he was writing his epic of the wheat and was calling for the social responsibility of the novelist, he was grinding out weak, Kiplingesque short stories to keep the pot boiling. Norris, unlike Stephen Crane, never renounced the "clever school" of literature as far as the short story was concerned. Thus, though *Vandover* and *McTeague* are not foreshadowed by Norris' early stories, he might nevertheless have been slowly evolving toward these novels during his California years.

Another way of accounting for the "explosion" of the two novels is to realize that Norris could admire a writer and borrow from him without necessarily sharing that writer's central vision of life. Because Norris often adopted Davis' offhand manner, or Kipling's display of technical knowledge, or Stevenson's narrative pace, or a whole host of Zola's techniques does not mean that one has to find room in Norris' fundamental beliefs for all the ideas of these writers. Norris was always receptive to literary influence, but he responded selectively to the ideas of other writers

Sneed, Lavin & O'Malley

INC.

INC. hears that . . .

Architects from a major Chicago firm are close to tying up financing for a floating casino/celebrity drug-alcohol treatment center to be anchored off Navy Pier. . . . Rock stars **Madonna** and **Prince** have been offered major roles in a pilot for a TV sitcom loosely based on Henry David Thoreau's "Walden." . . . **Elizabeth Taylor** and "Dynasty" designer **Nolan Miller** are working on a "matronly" wardrobe for her introduction into the series as **Joan Collins'** mother. . . . You can fool some of the people some of the time, except on April 1.

The envelope, please . . .

● New York Gov. **Mario Cuomo** recently won a presidential straw poll among Iowa Democratic activists. The poll gave 73 percent to Cuomo, against 15 percent to **Gary Hart** and 8 percent to Sen. **Ted Kennedy** [D., Mass.]. And in a Capitol Hill poll of Democratic congressional staff . . .

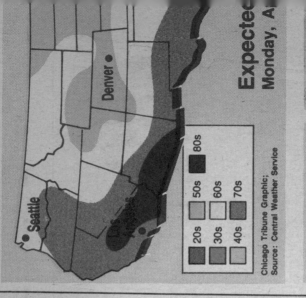

Expected
Monday, A

20s 50s 80s
30s 60s
40s 70s

Chicago Tribune Graphic;
Source: Central Weather Service

Frontal clouds extend from
Gulf to low pressure center
over northern Illinois.
Thick clouds are causing

in accordance with his own temperament. Out of the variety of writers who attracted him during his undergraduate years he gradually shaped a literary mode which was both derivative and personal.

We have noticed that Norris' earliest work, *Yvernelle*, revealed his fondness for the sensationalism and moralism afforded by the conventions of the medieval romance. Kipling's appeal was that of his fresh, zestful incorporation of these strains in a modern setting—though not in the middle- and lower-class world Norris was to use in his novels. Kipling's India is exotic, and so are the backgrounds of several of Norris' earliest Kiplingesque stories, such as "The Finding of Lieutenant Outhwaite" (March 13, 1891) and "The Son of a Sheik" (June 1, 1891). Norris was also much taken by Richard Harding Davis at this time. Although Davis used many of Kipling's techniques and was often called the American Kipling, he set most of his stories in his own cities of New York and Philadelphia. It was therefore probably the combined influence of Kipling and Davis which encouraged Norris to use a contemporary San Francisco background for a number of stories which he wrote during 1890-1894.

Enter now Le Conte and enter also Zola at about the same time or a little later. Le Conte's impact is most obvious in "Lauth" (March, 1893), as I have shown. In this story Norris for the last time used a medieval setting. He apparently felt that in order to dramatize the theme of man's ethical duality he needed a scene permitting both extreme violence and didactic allegory, and that a medieval setting of warfare and cabalistic experiment would be most easily adaptable to those needs. "Lauth" resembles such popular works of Norris' day as Stevenson's *Dr. Jekyll and Mr. Hyde* (1886) and Oscar Wilde's *The Picture of Dorian Gray* (1891). These are didactic romances in which mysterious and supernatural potions and portraits play major roles in allegorical representations of man's ethical duality. "Each of us has Heaven and Hell in him," says Dorian Gray, echoing Dr. Jekyll's cry that man is "not truly one, but truly two." "Lauth" also allegorizes this theme, but does so within Norris' own framework of Le Contean ideas and a medieval setting.

Zola's major attraction was that he sensationally portrayed within a contemporary setting that which Norris above all responded to in Le Conte's ideas at this time—the theme that man contains within himself powerful animal forces which often lead him to violence or degradation. Norris was always to stress in his discussions of Zola not that Zola professed a creed of materialistic determinism (he almost entirely ignored this idea),[5] but that Zola was engrossed in the passionate and violent in life, in "the extraordinary, the vast, the monstrous, and the tragic."[6] Le Conte had supplied Norris with ways of thinking about the reality and role of the brute in man, and now Zola showed him that these themes could be made the stuff of an exciting fiction set in a local, contemporary world. Both the sensational treatment of the beast in man of "Lauth" and the tendency toward the local and the modern in Norris' other short stories are also present in Zola. No wonder that Norris was seldom without his paperback Zola novel during his last years at Berkeley.

But Norris' immense attraction for Zola—and I have said nothing of his admiration for Zola's technical proficiency[7]—does not mean that he fully accepted Zola's view of human nature. "Lauth" dramatizes the reality of man's brute instincts and of his material nature, but its theme is also the primacy of the soul. Zola, despite his abhorrence for the sensual and the sexually promiscuous, both explicitly and implicitly rejected the idea of ethical duality. Human character to Zola was a matter of a physiologically describable temperament, and temperament was the product of such natural forces as heredity and environment.

He was to study man, he has his Zolaesque novelist say in *L'Oeuvre*, not as "this metaphysical marionette they've made us believe he is, but the physiological human being, determined by his surroundings, motivated by the functioning of his organs."[8] In this preface to *Thérèse Raquin* he explained that "Thérèse and Laurent are human animals, nothing more. I tried to follow, step by step, the hidden depths of passion, the urges of instinct and the mental unbalance resulting from an emotional crisis." Their remorse at the end of the novel "consists of a bodily disorder, the rebellion of a nervous system screwed to breaking point. The soul is not involved. . . ."[9]

When Norris came to write *Vandover* and *McTeague*, the various influences which I have described sorted themselves out according to his needs and ideas at that time. He rejected the "clever" writers—Kipling and Davis—for *Vandover* and *McTeague* were to be serious novels. Under the influence of Zola, whose technique of documentation he implicitly absorbed, he "researched" his novels to find scientific support for his ethical preconceptions. He thus substituted contemporary medical and psychological beliefs for the potions of allegory, though these beliefs clothe the same evolutionary ethical dualism present in "Lauth." One way of crudely describing the genesis of *Vandover* and *McTeague* is to say that Norris combines in them a Zolaesque documented sensationalism with Le Conte's evolutionary interpretation of the conventional theme of man's ethical duality.

2

At one time it was thought that Norris began writing *McTeague* during his last year at California, that he continued work on it at Harvard, and that he then put it aside for *Vandover*. It is now almost certain that though *McTeague* may have been conceived during 1893-94 (its central incident derives from a San Francisco murder of October, 1893), it was not begun until Norris reached Harvard. "Finishing year at Harvard, class of '95—McTeague begun this year," he wrote in a letter of 1900.[10] Moreover, his extant Harvard themes reveal that he worked primarily on *Vandover* in the fall of 1894 and on *McTeague* in the spring of 1895.[11] *Vandover* was probably finished by the end of the year, but *McTeague*, though planned and perhaps complete in a rough draft, was not finished until late 1897. Much of the writing of both novels occurred in English 22, the writing course that Norris took during his Harvard year, which makes it necessary to say something about the possible influence of his teacher, Lewis E. Gates, on the two works.

English 22 had about 250 students the year Norris was enrolled, and was given by Gates and three assistants.[12] The class met three times a week, with class work consisting largely of Gates' comments on student papers. Written work involved a short daily (that is, tri-weekly) theme on a subject "chosen by the student, who is advised to choose matters that he observes from day to day,"[13] and fortnightly themes of some length. The fortnightly themes were on assigned subjects for the first semester of the course, and on a single topic arranged between the instructor and the student in the second semester. (Norris, however, as an older, special student may have been given permission to write his fortnightly themes on his own subjects throughout the year.) The year's work culminated in a long project written in six weekly installments. For purposes of correcting themes and advising students, the class was divided into sections, with an assistant in charge of each. One of the assistants during Norris' year was William Vaughn Moody (who had replaced Robert Morss Lovett), but Norris' section assistant was Herbert V. Abbott, later a professor of English at Smith.

Of Norris' work in English 22, only the daily themes seem to have survived, and many of these are brief and ephemeral, though they do suggest something of the composition of the two novels. The fortnightly themes were probably chapters of the novels, and were therefore destroyed by Norris as he revised them into a finished text. There is little evidence that Gates read much of Norris' work for the course, since all the comments on his daily themes are by Abbott, and since section assistants also read the fortnightly themes. However, in a letter to Gates in 1899, Norris referred to Gates reading *McTeague* in its "embryonic form" as a fortnightly theme, which suggests that he asked Gates to read some portion of his work.[14] That Norris never met Gates does not preclude this possibility, for Gates was a withdrawn, distant man who communicated even with his assistants by letter.

I have earlier attempted to show that Norris came to Harvard fully armed with the intellectual and literary ideas which were to be given form in *Vandover* and *McTeague*. Yet he dedicated *McTeague* to Gates, not Le Conte or Zola, and wrote thanking him for his encouragement and criticism and naming him "God-father and sponsor" of the novel.[15] How, then, did Gates affect Norris' work?[16] First, Gates was finely sensitive to literary technique and form. His classes—in which he discussed these matters from student themes—were, as Norris later remembered,[17] absorbing to a young writer who desired "to be thoroughly prepared for a literary profession." Moreover, Gates endorsed a literary mode which Norris had come to Harvard prepared to attempt, and gave that mode a particularly autobiographical turn which is important for *Vandover*. Gates encouraged his students to deal with the world around them, and to do so primarily from their own point of view. His critical essays reveal this first emphasis in his thinking about literature, as for example in his praise of Mrs. Browning's *Aurora Leigh* for its realism. He admired the poem because "everywhere the reader is kept within sound of the busy rumour of daily life; he breathes the actual air of the smokey London streets; he explores squalid tenements; he watches the pageantry of church weddings . . .; he is never for long allowed to lose sight of the expressive visage of the great world of fact."[18] Gates found, however, that in general the post-romantics

> lacked the microscopic eye and the ingenious instinct for detail that are characteristic of the modern artist and of the modern commentator on life. It remained for the scientific spirit with its fine loyalty to fact, and for realism with its delicate sense of the world of the passing moment—for the *phase*—to carry still further the return to the regions of the Actual.[19]

But Gates required not only that literature be devoted to the "great world of fact," but also that it be derived from the author's personal knowledge and experience of fact. To the young writer in college, this dual emphasis leads almost directly to autobiographical college fiction, that is, to his own personal "region of the actual" of the moment. So Charles Flandrau, who took Gates' course in 1892-93, wrote *Harvard Episodes* (1897), and Reginald Kauffman, who took it in 1896-97, *Jarvis of Harvard* (1901). Indeed, these two works were too "factual" for many readers of the time, and both were attacked because of their depiction of the realities of undergraduate life.[20] It is, perhaps, not surprising that the novel which Norris started in the fall of 1894 begins with the experiences of a young man from San Francisco at Harvard.

Gates' general influence on Norris, therefore, was to encourage Norris' tendency toward fiction of a modern temper, leaning toward the autobiographical, and to encourage devotion to craft. Moreover, Norris felt in Gates' class a sympathy with and interest in original work which had been lacking at California and which Norris apparently needed at this point in his career. "The literary courses of the University of California do not develop literary instincts among the students who attend them," he wrote in 1896. "They order this matter better at Harvard," he went on,[21] and it was perhaps primarily his appreciation for this "better order" which prompted his great sense of indebtedness to Gates.

3

Although *Vandover and the Brute* was Norris' first novel, it was not published until 1914, twelve years after his death. The circumstances of its composition and publication are cloudy and complex, yet they have to be discussed in order to clear the way for an analysis of the novel as we know it.

Norris' Harvard themes suggest that the novel was complete by the end of the year. His theme of November 19, 1894, is from chapter IV of the eighteen-chapter novel, and that of January 4, 1895, is from chapter IX. In early April he published in the *Harvard Advocate* a short descriptive sketch called "The End of the Act" from chapter XIV. It is also clear that he revised the work after leaving Harvard, though his brief original notes for the novel indicate that he made few, if any, major changes when revising.[22] Some of his Harvard themes containing *Vandover* material are printed verbatim in the novel, but others undergo stylistic revisions of one kind or another. Although the facsimile title page of the novel which Charles Norris published in 1914 bears the date 1895,[23] these revisions seem to be of 1896, and were probably made on the original manuscript, as was Norris' custom. The year 1896 is the best possibility for this revision because Norris mentions twice the imminent opening of the Sutro Baths, which occurred early in 1896 amidst much fanfare (V, 248, 260).* That the revision was completed by November, 1897, is revealed by the version of "The End of the

---

* Citations from Norris' novels refer to *The Complete Edition of Frank Norris* (Garden City, N. Y., 1928), and appear in the text whenever possible.

Act" which he published then in the San Francisco *Wave*.[24] This version is slightly revised from that of the *Advocate*, but it is the one which appears in the novel.

It is not known whether Norris submitted the novel to a publisher either before or shortly after revising it. When *McTeague* appeared in early 1899, however, he offered *Vandover* to his publisher, Doubleday and McClure. This firm, which had hesitated over *McTeague* for a year, rejected *Vandover*, though they sent it to William Heinemann for possible publication in England. When Heinemann also refused the novel because it was too "advanced," Norris apparently despaired of publishing it,[25] since he began lifting scenes from it, including the ubiquitous "The End of the Act," for other novels.[26]

In his foreword to the 1914 edition of *Vandover and the Brute*, Charles G. Norris, Frank's brother, explained that the manuscript had been lost in the confusion of the San Francisco fire of 1906 and had come to light in 1913. In a conversation with Franklin Walker on June 9, 1930, however, Charles said that the manuscript had been held for several years by Jeannette Norris (Frank's widow), and that the fire story was not authentic.[27] Denison Cliff's report in 1907 that the novel was being considered by a New York publisher supports Charles' later account.[28] The most probable history of the novel between 1902 and 1914 is that it was initially withheld by Jeannette Norris because of its sensational autobiographical elements, and that it was then submitted several times by Charles until Doubleday no longer found it too advanced for publication. The fire story was used to explain the long delay between Norris' death and the novel's publication.

Charles also told Franklin Walker that in preparing the novel for publication he had made some cuts—primarily a long chapter early in the novel in which Vandover is drunk, and a description of a parlor used in *Blix*—and had added about 5,000 words.[29] Now

5,000 words are quite a lot, even in a novel of approximately 100,000 words. Charles could not remember what kind of additions he made, and it is possible that he overestimated them. His memory could be faulty in such matters, for in 1914 he reported that the manuscript showed signs of much revision (borne out by the facsimile page he published),[30] while in 1931 he told Walker that it had been a clean copy.[31] Moreover, if Norris had submitted the novel to at least two publishers, it is probable that it was in reasonably finished form, and that Charles' primary editorial role was to cut objectional and repetitious material. I can find no passages which are alien to Norris' style or thought, so Charles made either expert additions or none.

The novel, as we know it today, was written during 1894-95, revised in 1896, and again revised, probably slightly, by Charles after Frank's death. For all practical purposes, we may consider *Vandover* as basically of 1894-95 and as totally by Frank Norris.

4

Vandover is Norris' most autobiographical novel. *Blix* is a more literal account of one phase of his life, but it reveals less of the inner man. In *Vandover* Norris dramatized many of his basic worries about himself, doing so within the double context of Le Conte's ideas and Zola's studies of degeneracy. The full title of the novel reflects some of these sources and motives. Charles Norris shortened the title to *Vandover and the Brute*, but the original title page contains the subtitle "A Study of Life and Manners in an American City at the End of the Nineteenth Century."[32] Together, the title and subtitle suggest Zola's usual combined portrayal of an abnormal, flawed character and a detailed social background, but the main title stresses the ethical duality of the central character.

33

The autobiographical element is clear from the beginning. Vandover, a young man of good family, is brought to San Francisco when a child, as was Norris. His father, like Norris', is retired but speculates in real estate. Both young men have undergraduate careers (Vandover at Harvard) and then attempt a life of art—Vandover as a painter, Norris as a writer. Norris' friends recalled that while at Berkeley he took a lively role in the usual fraternity activities of gambling, drinking, and sexual exploration.[33] It is probably Norris' concern about this side of his nature, and perhaps also about his distaste for physical effort, which he projected into a study of Vandover's ten years after Harvard, a period during which Vandover degenerates physically and mentally because of his sensuality and pliability.

The name Vandover has autobiographical implications. Norris had been influenced at Berkeley by Davis' stories about a fashionable young man named Van Bibber. Two of Norris' early stories contain a parallel character, Vandover. One of them, "The Finding of Lieutenant Outhwaite" (March 13, 1891), uses the device of a Kiplingesque autobiographical narrator who tells an unusual yarn to a friend. The narrator is called Vandover, which suggests that Norris had begun to identify himself with the name and character. In the other story, "The Way of the World" (July 26, 1892), Vandover is a young man around town. When Norris turned to a novel about the degeneration of a young San Francisco artist, he was probably attracted to the name Vandover because of its dual connotations of the autobiographical and the San Francisco worldly.

Norris quickly sketched Vandover's youth and his Harvard years. Most of the novel is concerned with the gradual conquest of Vandover's spiritual nature by his brute nature during the decade after his return to San Francisco. Vandover's decline, however, is not simply that of a man who allows the animal in him to gain the upper hand. Rather, his fall results from weaknesses in his character which are closely related to Le Conte's idea of the twofold potential of man's animal heritage. Not only does Vandover fail to repress his sensual nature, but he also fails to exert his brute strength to compete in the struggle for existence. His flaw is not that brute sensuality is initially more powerful in him than in other men, but that he too easily succumbs to that in his environment which caters to sensual pleasure and that he lacks the force to pursue a way of life antithetical to such pleasures. " 'What's a good man if he's weak?' " Norris was later to have Blix ask Condy Rivers (III, 56). It is this lack of strength which causes Vandover to sink to the lowest level in his San Francisco world and to be all but destroyed by the law of nature which weeds out the weak in order to drive the race forward. Throughout the novel, then, Norris either states or dramatizes Vandover's "pliable nature" and his "fatal adaptability to environment which he had permitted himself to foster throughout his entire life" (V, 278).[34] Put in nonevolutionary terms, the novel is about a weak man who gradually loses the best influences in his world and yields to the worst in that world and in his own nature.

Norris makes the causes of Vandover's fall doubly clear by counterposing against his decline the rise of a character who has opposite qualities. Charlie Geary, like Vandover, enjoys sensual pleasures. But, unlike Vandover, he recognizes the reality of the struggle for existence, and he has the force to push forward rather than halt at the accessible pleasure of the moment. As Vandover's motif, repeated again and again, is his pliable, too adaptable nature, so Geary's is "Every man for himself."[35] As Vandover always postpones effort and conflict, so Geary resists all that interferes with the achievement of his goals, and seeks "to attain the desired object in spite of the whole world, to ride on at it, trampling down or smashing through everything that stood in the way . . ." (V, 288). The novel begins with the two men class-mates at Harvard. It ends with Geary a rising young lawyer, poli-tician, and real estate owner, Vandover a broken, semi-idiotic derelict.

But the novel is more than a combination of a puritan code of work and self-control and Dr. Jekyll's discovery that man is not one but two. For just as the appeal of Stevenson's novel lies in the sensational physical reality of Dr. Jekyll and Mr. Hyde, so *Vandover* derives much of its strength from Norris' ability to create exciting concrete equivalents of his moral abstractions. Where Stevenson had worked with mysterious potions and transfigurations, Norris—like Zola—drew upon contemporary scientific belief for the images in which to clothe his abstractions.

In the course of the novel Vandover acquires an illness which eventually turns him into a shattered wreck. It has been generally assumed that his illness is lycanthropy, a rare mental disease in which the victim believes he is a wolf, since that is Vandover's most sensational symptom.[36] Critics of the novel have had dif-ficulty establishing a causal link between Vandover's vices and this disease. They have attacked Norris, not so much for assign-ing Vandover a disease which symbolizes his decline to animality, as for arbitrarily blaming the disease on Vandover's brute nature. It has not been realized that Vandover has general paralysis of the insane (also called paresis or softening of the brain), a disease which may include lycanthropy as one of its symptoms. Today we know that general paralysis is caused by syphilitic infection of the brain. In the late nineteenth century, however, though syphilis was often mentioned as a possible cause, it was more commonly believed that intemperate sexual and drinking habits were the primary causes.[37]

Vandover's illness conforms to the description of general paralysis found in the standard texts on insanity of Norris' day.[38]

Vandover has led a debauched life of sexual and alcoholic excess in San Francisco. He also has had sexual relations with the prostitute Flossie, who during the same period gave syphilis to young Dolly Haight. The symptoms of the first stage of general paralysis include slight incoordination of the finer muscular movements, intermittent dull headache, tenseness, insomnia, gradually increasing disregard for conventional standards of behavior, and suicidal melancholy. Such are Vandover's initial symptoms when the disease makes its appearance some five years after his return from Harvard. He first becomes aware that he is ill when he is unable to draw.[39] From this prodromal stage, during which the patient is seldom recognized by his friends as insane, the disease pursues a long road downward to complete mental and physical dissolution and death.

General paralysis was believed to take one of two possible psychological forms—mental depression or exaltation. Vandover suffers from depression, and the melancholic hallucinations which are an important symptom of this form of the disease as it progresses are in his case those of lycanthropy.[40] Norris deviates from the standard descriptions of the disease, however, in making Vandover's hallucinations coherent and consistent, since most authorities agreed that they are usually mixed and disordered. His deviation in this detail reveals his desire to find a striking symbol for the relationship between the cause of the disease and its symptoms. Man as a snarling wolf was a sensational symbol of man's surrender to the brute within.

As the disease advances, Vandover suffers most of its other major symptoms—attacks of hallucinatory dementia; occasional loss of consciousness; constant dull headache; gradual loss of memory and power of attention; and increased physical slovenliness and moral turpitude. When we last see Vandover, some ten years after his return from Harvard, he has reached the stage at which the disease is usually recognized and the patient confined. (A lengthy prodromal period was one of the important characteristics of general paralysis.) He now has little mental ability; his hands shake violently; his speech wanders; he can perform only routine physical tasks. He is fast approaching the "vegetative" stage which precedes death.

I have not been able to discover an exact source for Norris' knowledge of general paralysis. He tended to rely either on friends or on books for exact information, using books as a second choice. A possible personal source of information about the disease (and also for some ideas used in *McTeague*) was Dr. William M. Lawlor, an old family friend. Dr. Lawlor, whom Norris publicly defended in 1902 against charges of mistreating patients in a state mental home, was a specialist in public health and mental illness. He had studied at Bellevue and had held public health posts in San Francisco, and would have been thoroughly familiar with the disease.[41] Norris could have consulted him before leaving San Francisco for Harvard, or could have confirmed his facts after his return.

The disease of general paralysis is a major element in the moral rationale of the novel. It was believed that in general paralysis, unlike most mental diseases, heredity played little or no role. Norris can portray Vandover as responsible for his decline because Vandover has yielded to the brute within him and that surrender has caused the disease which destroys him. Here is poetic justice with the exactitude of the absolute moralist and the sensational symbolist. Vandover's animal tendencies ultimately cause him to become animal-like, both in the major characteristics of his disease (gradual degeneration to brute-like insensitivity and coarseness) and in its principal dramatic symptom (lycanthropic hallucinations). Norris' choice of the wolf as his symbol of sensual animality probably owes less to a particular literary source—though both Kipling and Zola use it—than to the general cultural association of the werewolf with possession by the devil. The disease of general paralysis was thus primarily a means of naturalizing the conventional religious belief that the devil works through the senses; in other words, it served as a natural explanation for a religious preconception. Vandover's lycanthropy is psychologically valid. A paresis patient who believes that his disease has been caused by his sensual appetites may very well suffer attacks of lycanthropic hallucinations. But when Vandover recalls during one of his attacks that "He had told himself that he did not believe in a hell. Could there be a worse hell than this? (V, 213), we recognize that for Norris scientific fact was primarily a means toward a moral end.

Norris was not content that the theme of the novel be merely that a weak, sensual man will cause his own destruction. Norris at his best had a sense of detail matched by few American novelists, but he also had a fondness for the grandiose, for the sweeping general idea which embodies all experience. He was therefore often moved to relate individual experience to larger forces, to relate a man in love, for example, to the role of love as a beneficent force in the world. Some of his poorest writing, and occasionally some of his best, stems from this tendency, since cosmic forces lend themselves to rhetoric but not to the sense of actuality necessary in most fiction. In order to gain this sense of actuality when depicting cosmic forces, and also to infuse them with an emotional vitality, Norris often used a repetitive concrete metaphor, a device which sometimes muddies the logic of the natural law he is attempting to describe. Midway in *Vandover* Norris introduced the existence of a vast force operative in human life. Vandover, as he looks over the city from his window, senses this force:

39

It was Life, the murmur of the great, mysterious force that spun the wheels of Nature and that sent it onward like some enormous engine, resistless, relentless; an engine that sped straight forward, driving before it the infinite herd of humanity, driving it on at breathless speed through all eternity, driving it no one knew whither, crushing out inexorably all those who lagged behind the herd and who fell from exhaustion; grinding them to dust beneath its myriad iron wheels, riding over them, still driving on the herd that yet remained, driving it recklessly, blindly on and on toward some far-distant goal, some vague, unknown end, some mysterious, fearful bourne forever hidden in thick darkness (V, 202).

The metaphor of the engine is that of the struggle for existence which grinds down some while pushing the mass of the race forward. A key issue is the relationship of Vandover and Geary to this struggle: are they pawns and ciphers in a mechanistic system, or do they choose their own fates? This question is answered by parallel passages describing the engine in relation to the two characters. Vandover, at the point when he first realizes the severity of his symptoms and fears that he is "going mad," is described as follows:

It was the punishment that he had brought upon himself, some fearful nervous disease, the result of his long indulgence of vice, his vile submission to the brute that was to destroy his reason; some collapse of all his faculties, beginning first with that which was highest, most sensitive—his art—spreading onward and downward till he should have reached the last stages of idiocy. It was Nature inexorably exacting. It was the vast fearful engine riding him down beneath its myriad spinning wheels, remorsely, irresistibly (V, 213).

Vandover has by his vice contracted a disease which has made him one of the "laggards" in the "herd" of humanity and therefore one of the victims of the struggle for existence. The disease of general paralysis is thus an agent of evolutionary progress, since it removes from the "herd" one who has "faltered"—that is, who has regressed to a brute sensuality and who lacks the necessary drive to keep pace with the herd.

Now what of Geary, who, unlike Vandover, controls his sensual indulgences and through shrewdness, industry, and trickery is fast rising to wealth and prominence? At the close of the novel, Geary muses over his success and Vandover's fall:

> Every man for himself—that was his maxim. It might be damned selfish, but it was human nature: the weakest to the wall, the strongest to the front. . . . Vast, vague ideas passed slowly across the vision of his mind, ideas that could hardly be formulated into thought, ideas of the infinite herd of humanity, driven on as if by some enormous, relentless engine, driven on toward some fearful distant bourne, driven on recklessly at headlong speed. All life was but a struggle to keep from under those myriad spinning wheels that dashed so close behind. Those were happiest who were farthest to the front. To lag behind was peril; to fall was to perish, to be ridden down, to be beaten to the dust, to be inexorably crushed and blotted out beneath that myriad of spinning iron wheels. Geary looked up quickly and saw Vandover standing in the doorway (V, 288-89).

The dialectic of the novel, then, is that within the struggle for existence permeating all life the animal nature of man exerts itself in two ways. A Vandover, surrendering to the sensual, will lag behind and be crushed. A Geary, exploiting a brute force to push ahead, will be in the forefront of the herd and will escape such agents of the struggle as disease and poverty. Thus, though Vandover is crushed by vast, resistless forces, the blame is his because he chose a mode of life which led to that fate. The flaw underlying his choice involves two interdependent weaknesses, both of which function within an evolutionary ethical scheme. Man must resist the sensual, and he must have the strength to resist the pressure of environment, since man has the unique capacity to control rather than be controlled by his environment. If man succumbs to either of these two vestiges of his animal past, he handicaps himself in the evolutionary struggle, and his self-imposed destruction soon follows.

The novel therefore poses a moral dilemma. Is Norris implying that Geary's code of dog-eat-dog is best, that without the ideal of "every man for himself" the individual "lags behind" and is eventually crushed by a combination of his weaknesses, his environment, and his fellow men? He seems to suggest this, for Vandover not only gives in to his own pliability and sensuality, but is tricked and cheated by Geary. Norris' ethical scheme is incompletely dramatized in *Vandover*, however, and is at odds with both his sympathies and his ideas. He knows that the Vandovers fall and that the Gearys rise, but his sympathies are all with the Vandovers. Though he explicitly castigates Vandover, and has Vandover castigate himself, Norris' identification of himself with Vandover makes him a pathetic figure. Geary, on the other hand, is too much a scheming, self-preoccupied character to attract any warmth. In chapter IV, for example, when the drunken Ellis gets the three of them into a fight, Geary cautiously retires while Vandover remains. Geary's is the wiser action, but Vandover's the more generous and appealing.

In later novels Norris again presented characters of great force and drive. But he portrayed them as deficient until they acquired a spiritual nature, which he represented as a compassionate understanding of the needs and feelings of others. Geary may have the necessary force to survive in the struggle for existence, but he lacks the spiritual half of the Le Contean dualism, that which makes man distinctly human. Geary and Vandover are polar extremes. At the close of the novel Vandover is all pliability, Geary all strength, Vandover all sensual beast, Geary all brute force. Neither has the correct balance or hierarchy of qualities demanded by Le Conte. The novel is flawed, then, because Norris' desire to create a foil to Vandover's deficiencies results in a character who incorrectly implies a standard as well as a foil. Norris' emotional coloring of the two characters only partially compensates for this flaw.

Vandover has an intertwined double structure, with most of its incidents and symbols playing some role in the forward movement of this twofold pattern. First, there is the structure of Vandover's fall and Geary's rise, dominated by the engine metaphor. Secondly, there is the structure of the change within Vandover as he moves from the awakening of the brute until it completely dominates him. The second is the more fully developed pattern, and it embodies most of the novel's scenes, characters, and symbols. It particularly involves the animal imagery which at first appears only slightly but which finally is the novel's major source of metaphor and symbol. This second structure allegorizes most of the novel's subsidiary characters, since they represent forces contributing to one or the other of Vandover's two natures. Turner Ravis and Vandover's father ("the Old Gentleman") are the Good Woman and Home, while Ellis and Flossie are Gambling and Lust. As the novel proceeds, the spirit-supporting characters have less and less influence on Vandover and disappear from the scene; Ellis and his world, however, have increasingly prominent roles. Norris also used Vandover's dwellings to plot his decline, as we follow him from his father's house to his luxurious flat, to hotel rooms, and finally into the street. These changes symbolize material equivalents of Vandover's moral state and his fatal pliability, for he quickly accommodates himself to any environment.

In addition to these dynamic symbols, Norris also established several pairs of more or less static symbols to represent the struggle within Vandover's dual nature. These pairs are static in the sense that they function throughout the novel as moral reference points, alluded to again and again, though they do not always appear concretely. One obvious pair is Flossie and Turner: "Turner Ravis influenced [Vandover] upon his best side, calling out in him all that was cleanest, finest, and most delicate. Flossie appealed only to the animal and the beast in him, the evil, hideous brute that made instant answer" (V, 44). Norris here reveals something basic in his writing—his tendency toward over-simplified moral absolutes. When he attempts to describe or analyze mental and moral states, he scarcely seems to warrant serious attention. Yet when he creates a pictorial or dramatic equivalent of his analysis, he is a very different writer. For example, chapters III and IV constitute an exercise in contrast, since we follow Vandover from a Saturday evening party at Turner's to a debauch later that night at the Imperial Bar (where he sees Flossie) and on the town. Norris brings alive the opposing moral climate of Turner's world and Flossie's, and climaxes the contrast strikingly when he has the still drunk Vandover take communion with Turner on Sunday morning. He makes believable within these chapters the idea that Turner might be a good influence on Vandover and Flossie a bad one, but he does much more. He creates a world of actuality, and because actuality is subtle and complex, there exists a wide gap between that world and Norris' raw, simplified analysis of it.

He is more successful with two other pairs of symbols which are primarily dramatic. The best pair is that of the Imperial Bar and Paris. Norris places much of the novel's action at the Imperial. It is where Vandover begins his first important debauch, where he seduces Ida Wade, and where he often goes with Ellis and the Dummy. Norris establishes the Imperial both as a vividly concrete reality and as a controlled, recurring symbol, and his ability in this respect is one of the major strengths of the novel. Although Vandover spends much time at the Imperial, he often plans to go to Paris, where he will begin his art career seriously. The two symbols are thus dramatically juxtaposed throughout the novel. Several times Vandover is about to cast off his San Francisco world and go to Paris, but instead drifts back to the Imperial.

The last important symbolic pair are the two flats Vandover has to choose between after his father's death, when he is determined to throw off the brute and return to his art. One flat symbolizes art and sensual deprivation, since it has an excellent studio but a small, dark sitting room. The other is more expensive, and has a poor studio and a warm, comfortable sitting room. Vandover chooses the second, and soon returns to passivity and dissipation.

Vandover's decline, after his return from Harvard, is not one steep grade downward. He tries several times to pull up sharply and change his way of life, and these attempts divide the novel into numerous sections of decline and plateau. Seen in wider focus, however, the work has three main divisions. The first seven chapters describe Vandover's youth and the first three and a half years of his life in San Francisco. During this time his basic character traits appear and he is on the road to dissolution. This section concludes with the suicide of Ida Wade, the middle-class girl Vandover has seduced and made pregnant. Chapters VIII and IX, in the middle of the novel, describe Vandover's boat trip to Coronado and back. These chapters seem to have little relationship to his decline, but are actually important. On his return, he loses first his father (who dies partly from the shock of learning of Vandover's affair with Ida) and then Turner (who is sufficently affected by the affair to break off their waning romance). Vandover now sinks fully into a life of drink, gambling, and "disreputable houses" which culminates in the disease that first removes his final spiritual prop—his art—and then all but destroys him.

Vandover's sea voyage comes at a moment when he has vowed to reform and still has the strength and some of the supports necessary to do so. On the voyage he has experiences which demonstrate those aspects of his animal nature which he must change if he is to lead a new life on his return. First, on the way to Coronado he meets Grace Irving, an attractive girl eager to be picked up. He fights the temptation to do so, however, and recognizes that he is still able to control his sensual nature. On his return voyage, his ship, the *Mazatlan*, is wrecked.

> Vandover's very first impulse was a wild desire of saving himself; he had not the least thought for anyone else. Every soul on board might drown, so only he should be saved. It was the primitive animal instinct, the blind adherence to the first great law, an impulse that in this first moment of excitement could not be resisted (V, 112).

The ship goes down, and in the ensuing chaos a man attempts to climb aboard Vandover's overloaded lifeboat, jeopardizing the lives of those already in it. They unite to beat him off, and he drowns. "It was the animal in them all that had come to the surface in an instant, the primal instinct of the brute striving for its life and for the life of its young" (V, 122). These shipwreck incidents document the struggle for existence in two ways. They prove that even Vandover, despite his usual passivity, can at moments of crisis exert a brute force to save himself, and that this universal instinct for self-preservation results in the destruction of those who threaten the well-being of the mass. In the course of the voyage, therefore, Vandover has learned three things: that he can control his sensual nature, that he has a potential of brute strength, and that the struggle for existence is indeed a terrible engine grinding down the laggards. But he quickly discards these lessons, for his first action on landing is to eat at the Imperial. He responds once more to its good food and warmth, and even wishes that Flossie should come in.

The two structures of the novel often intermingle, of course, but nowhere more so than in the last chapter, in which Geary, now a successful landlord, hires the derelict Vandover to clean out some empty cottages. Geary, who had earlier preempted Turner and had cheated Vandover out of the land on which the cottages stand, is now also Vandover's employer. Norris has not only presented Geary's rise and Vandover's fall, but has united the two actions in Geary's manipulation and exploitation of Vandover. Moreover, our last vision of Vandover is of a passive, uncomplaining, unthinking creature crawling in the filth under a sink and taunted by a four-year-old child. He is now completely the brute—capable of existing in any circumstance, dumb and unfeeling. In the long closing scene in which the new tenants of a cottage mercilessly drive Vandover to extra task after extra task, until at last he is on hands and knees in the filth under the sink, the two structures dramatically and powerfully coalesce. Vandover is all brute, and he is being trod on and ground down by others.

One of the strengths of *Vandover* is Norris' ability to combine his "life and manners" material with his twofold structure. The long description of the workmen's cottages in the last chapter, for example, is one of a series of carefully depicted homes which ranges up and down the classes. Norris' "set scenes" also present a wide spectrum of San Francisco life—a dance party, a crowd at a fire, an opera performance, the Mechanics' Institute Fair, a college football crowd, and so on. These descriptions of interiors and of events serve a double role. First, they "populate" San Francisco—they create a sense of the real which on the one hand lends some of its feeling of probability to Vandover's degeneration, yet on the other hand contrasts vividly with the more sensational moments in that degeneration, as when the naked Vandover pads on all fours around his room while the college football crowd parades through the street. But also, as I have already partly indicated, they serve to document his decline, as in his transition from his father's imposing, well-ordered house to the dirt and smells of his room in the Reno House. Both Norris and Dreiser could capture with excellent detail the external reality of rooms, of clothing, of food, and of money, as though these were the fundamental realities of life. Yet both used this detail to symbolize the social position and the social longings which in a middle-class world are equivalent to moral and emotional states.

The novel is strongest, then, in making vividly real the decline of a weak man incapable of controlling his appetites or of rousing himself to fight the battle of life against his fellows or his environment. It is weakest when Norris attempts to make explicit the causes of this failure—that is, it is weakest in its two central symbols of the brute and of the engine. The primary trouble with the first is that it is overdone. Though a reader might not rebel at a dramatic presentation of a puritan attitude toward sex, indolence, or sensuality, he quickly wearies of that attitude in repetitive brute or wolf images and symbols. Norris' failure here is not of probability, since young men do get syphilis or become drunkards or ruin themselves gambling. It is rather a failure in taste, an incapacity to see that his constant analysis of the struggle in Vandover between his better and his brute nature is simplistic and tedious and is also an oblique moral lecture that most readers find objectionable. Norris did not realize that Vandover in the grip of fear because of his early symptoms, or Vandover asleep in the plaza or cleaning out beneath the sink, had far more ethical thrust than the oft-repeated rhetoric on "the animal in him, the brute, that would be fed, the evil, hideous brute grown now so strong that Vandover could not longer resist it. . ." (V, 285). Norris is here in part the victim of tendencies within his major sources. The excessive brute symbolism of *Vandover* was encouraged both by Le Conte's allegorical oversimplification of man's ethical nature and by Zola's technique of the massive, repetitive symbol or image which dominates a novel, such as the reproductive imagery in *La Terre*.

Norris' engine metaphor is also unsuccessful. He very carefully prepares the connection between the machine and death, first in the death of Vandover's mother as a railway engine thunders into a station, then in Vandover's recollection of her death on board the *Mazatlan* when he smells its engine oil. But despite this preparation, there is too great a gap between Vandover's specific disease and the generalization that nature is a destructive engine—the first a vivid physical reality, the second a totally different concrete image masking an abstraction. Norris was to have this difficulty several times during his career, and was to solve it satisfactorily only once—in *The Octopus*, when the wheat is both physical actuality and symbol of natural law.

In all, Norris was most powerful and suggestive when he abjured both explicit analysis and massive symbol for pictorial representation. There is more of the struggle for existence in Geary's careful scheming to get Vandover's land than in all the engine passages; there is more of Vandover's degeneration in the picture of him asleep in his own drunken vomit than in a dozen references to his brute nature. Throughout his career Norris praised Zola for his dramatic technique, for his removal of the authorial presence from the novel, and for his ability to allow a story to tell itself through scene and action. He never seems to have realized, however, that simplistic, loaded, and repetitious metaphors and symbols represented as much authorial presence

49

as a literal "I," and this failure accounts for much that is weak in his fiction, from *Vandover* to *The Pit*.

Vandover has other flaws, though none so important as those I have already discussed. It is occasionally tortuously plotted, as in the elaborate efforts required to give Dolly Haight a cut lip so that Flossie can infect him with her kiss. Indeed, the novel would be better if Haight were left out entirely. His syphilis—he has never slept with a woman, but has kissed Flossie once—embodies the supreme puritan sexual nightmare. It seems that Norris at one time intended to create a triad of characters within his evolutionary scheme. He was fond of using three characters or three groups of characters to establish theme (both *McTeague* and *The Octopus* rely on this device), and he began *Vandover* with Geary, Haight, and Vandover as three young men at Harvard and then in San Francisco. Haight is pure and moral, and though he occasionally visits the Imperial, he has full control of himself and is particularly susceptible to the moral influence of a good woman, such as Turner. Yet he is brought low by a stroke of chance. Norris probably wanted to indicate that chance as well as brute nature is a major factor in the struggle for existence. This theme is also suggested by the *Mazatlan* wreck, in which a Salvation Army lassie is killed fortuitously, and by the important role of chance in *McTeague*. But the theme is inadequately conceived and developed in *Vandover*. Haight's fall is more bathetic than tragic, and he plays only a minor role in the novel after its opening chapters.

Turner Ravis is perhaps the next most important character after Vandover and Geary. She is the first in a series of Norris' female characters whose function is to reinforce a man's moral strength and his dedication to a goal in life. Her failure to perform this duty is more Vandover's fault than hers. He has neglected and taken for granted her love for him until it fades and can no longer serve its moral role. She is almost completely a symbolic figure, like Vandover's father, and lacks reality and force. Many of Norris' characters throughout his work are of this kind. He is best with major figures, who take on a power and complexity from the fullness of their dramatic representation, and minor ones—such as Flossie or the Dummy—who have a limited and distinct role and can be vividly captured within that role. What one might call his "intermediate" characters are usually less successful because they are both too flat and too much in evidence.

Despite the variety of thematic and technical weaknesses I have sketched, *Vandover* compels interest, and if it is not a mature and controlled work of art, it is at least an absorbing one. It holds the reader in two interrelated ways, both of which I have already suggested. First, Vandover's fall is dramatically alive and convincing. When the tattered, broken wreck of a man says at the end of the novel, " 'My God! to think I was a Harvard man once!' " (V, 293), the statement may be ludicrous, but we are startled into realizing that indeed he was a Harvard man, that so powerful has been Norris' control of the gradation of his fall, and so convincing the physical reality of each step in his decline, that we have forgotten the distance that he has come. Secondly, Norris brings alive Vandover's fall by his use of the rich complexity of Vandover's San Francisco world and the concreteness of the "facts" of Vandover's disease. Norris works with ideas in his novels—an evolutionary ethical dualism is at the heart of *Vandover*'s theme—but the novel most succeeds when these ideas are experienced through scene and incident, when Norris' magnificent sense of the tactile reality of a room, or of the smell of a bar, or of the sweat of fear, shape themselves around these ideas. He was often to search for the "big idea," to be absorbed in cosmic systems. He was best, however, not when he neglected these (then his work sank to the trivial), but when he found a way to embody these ideas in the concrete detail of scene and incident that he could capture so well.

5

The initial inspiration for *McTeague* was probably a San Francisco murder in late 1893, when Norris was in his senior year at Berkeley and was deeply immersed in Zola's novels. A laborer named Collins, separated from his wife, stabbed her to death in the cloakroom of a kindergarten, for which she was the char-woman, when she refused him money.[42] Norris was no doubt intrigued by two aspects of the crime. First, the unusual setting for the murder, a kindergarten, was closely related to his mother's philanthropic activities. It was the custom for wealthy San Francisco society women to endow kindergartens, and Mrs. Norris had founded and continued to support the Lester Norris Memorial Kindergarten.[43] In *McTeague* Norris shifted the scene of the murder from Second and Folsom, where it had occurred, to Pacific Street, the location of the Lester Norris Kindergarten. He also introduced a number of "grand ladies of the Kindergarten Board" who are decorating the kindergarten for a children's festival (VIII, 315). His playfulness, however—which led him to describe himself in a scene at the Big Dipper Mine and to have Trina's dental appointments coincide with the meeting time of English 22[44]—did not extend to a portrayal of Mrs. Norris herself.

Besides the piquancy of the setting, Norris was attracted by the similarity of the murder to themes and incidents he was encountering in Zola. The newspaper accounts of Collins stressed that he was a drunken brute; "whenever he got drunk he beat [his wife] and if she did not give him money he knocked her down."[45]

Indeed, "brute" was the key word in the reports of Collins, an interpretation encouraged by the viciousness of the crime ("Twenty-Nine Fatal Wounds" ran one headline),[46] by Collins' dull-witted, inept attempts to conceal it, and by his lack of remorse. "Collins has the face of a brute," the *Examiner* noted, while the *Chronicle* stated that "Collins continues to bear himself with a stolid, brutish indifference that marks him as a type of all that is low in humanity."[47] In short, here was a vicious crime in a low-class setting involving drunkenness, poverty, and brutality—a combination characteristic of such Zola novels as *L'Assommoir, La Bête humaine, Thérèse Raquin,* and *Germinal.* "Terrible things must happen to the characters of the naturalistic tale," Norris wrote in June, 1896, referring to Zola's work at a time when *McTeague* was still incomplete. "They must be twisted from the ordinary, wrenched out from the quiet, uneventful round of every-day life, and flung into the throes of a vast and terrible drama that works itself out in unleased passions, in blood, and in sudden death."[48]

When Norris began writing *McTeague* at Harvard, he stressed those sensational elements common to both the Collins murder and Zola's novels. His Harvard themes on *McTeague*, eight in all, from January 7 to March 8, 1895, are primarily on McTeague's drunkenness, his brutal mistreatment of Trina, and his murder of her in the kindergarten. Norris' last theme, on March 8, is a plot summary:

McTeague who is a third class dentist in an uptown business street marries Trina a kindergarten teacher. Their misfortunes begin after a few years. McTeague, having no diploma, is forbidden to practice and begins to drink heavily. For a long time Trina supports the two, until she finally loses her place and in a short while the household falls into great poverty and misery. McTeague goes from bad to worse and finally ends by killing his wife. He manages to escape and goes back to the mines where the first part of his life has been spent. The facts concerning him come to light here and he is obliged to run for it. His way is across an arm of an Arizona desert. Here he is ridden down by a deputy sheriff. The two are sixty miles from the nearest human being and McTeague determines to fight, he kills the sheriff and is about to go on when he discovers that even in the fight the sheriff has managed to handcuff their wrists together. He is chained to the body sixty miles from help.[49]

Some details of the finished novel, such as McTeague's lack of a diploma and the fight in the desert, are in this early summary. One detail now present—that Trina is a kindergarten teacher—was to be changed. Absent entirely from the summary are several major segments or themes in the novel: the lengthy account of the courtship and early married life of Trina and McTeague, the theme of Trina's avarice, and the two subplots.

Norris apparently continued to work on *McTeague* during the spring of 1895, despite the fact that none of his extant themes after March 8 deal with the novel. On March 19 he drew out from the Harvard Library a book on dentistry from which he derived the technical dental details used in the novel.[50] Moreover, his letter to Lewis E. Gates, as well as his dedication to him, suggests that by the time he left Harvard he had carried *McTeague* beyond isolated scenes and a cursory plot summary.

How much of the novel he wrote at Harvard, however, is difficult to say. In his later accounts of *McTeague's* composition he said that though it was begun at Harvard, it was written in the fall of 1897, when he spent several months at the Placer County mine of his friend Seymour Waterhouse.[51] It is also uncertain whether he worked on *McTeague* between the late spring of 1895, after leaving Cambridge, and the fall of 1897. During this time he published three excerpts from *McTeague* in the *Wave*, but two of these appeared when he was rewriting the novel

(October and November, 1897) and the third is a description of McTeague's dental parlor which comes early in the work.[52] In any case, the extant pages of the manuscript of *McTeague* suggest that the novel was either completely revised or freshly composed in late 1897. This manuscript is primarily a clean copy, with some minor revisions, and served as printer's copy. It was undoubtedly the copy which Norris made just before or after he completed his stay in the Sierras, which he then submitted to Doubleday and McClure early in 1898, soon after he joined the firm.[53] The novel was "held up by Doubleday's hesitancy because of the realistic contents," one of the company's editors later recalled,[54] but it was finally published in February, 1899. There were some protests from readers and reviewers about the scene in the theatre in which "Owgooste" Sieppi suffers a physiological calamity not uncommon among young children, and the scene was revised in later issues. It does not appear in its original form in the *Complete Edition* republication of *McTeague*, but it was restored in a private press edition in 1941 and in most editions since then.

In the interval between early March, 1895, and October, 1897, *McTeague* continued to grow and take shape in Norris' mind, whether he worked extensively on it during this time or not. It emerged finally, in his revision of late 1897, as rather a different work from what is suggested by his 1895 plot summary. The major influences on the novel during this intervening period need to be traced, since they will help explain much in the finished work.

The Zola novels which had the greatest effect on the development of *McTeague* were *L'Assommoir* and *La Bête humaine*.[55] To the pivotal event of the Collins murder, Norris added much of the spirit and detail of *L'Assommoir*, including its love triangle, its plot movement of gradual decline after initial prosperity, and its detailed rendering of a middle- and lower-class milieu. It is possible to find traces of *L'Assommoir* throughout *McTeague*, from characterization (Lantier and Marcus, the initial suitors, are both intemperate radicals) to scene (a wedding feast) to plot (a crucial stroke of fate). But McTeague differs from the drunken Coupeau of *L'Assommoir* in two important ways—he commits a murder, and he himself is a brute of a man, huge, strong, dumb. In the characterization of McTeague, Norris appears to have been influenced primarily by the contemporary accounts of Collins and by Zola's portrait of an unrepentant vicious murderer in *La Bête humaine*. In that work Jacques Lantier, the victim of an inherited homicidal mania, stabs his mistress to death. What is particularly significant in the characterization of Lantier is that his mania is portrayed as an uncontrollable atavistic urge to kill any woman who arouses his sexual desire. The alcoholism and insanity of Lantier's forefathers have made him a "human beast," a man who exhibits psychological vestiges of the prehistoric savage. Moreover, though Lantier is neither stupid nor physically brutish, he does have a striking atavistic facial characteristic—a very prominent jaw.

Zola had dramatized the effects of inherited degeneracy throughout the Rougon-Macquart series, and his earlier *Thérèse Raquin* contains a brutish murderer. But in *La Bête humaine* he portrayed for the first time the instinctive homicidal criminal. In this portrait he was directly and acknowledgedly influenced by the late nineteenth-century school of criminal anthropology, and, more particularly, by Cesare Lombroso, the founder and leader of the school.[56] Lombroso's central and most widely disseminated belief was that the criminal is characterized by atavism resulting from degeneration of the nervous system, with alcohol one of the chief causes of that degeneration.[57] He held that criminals were members of a biological subspecies which was at an earlier stage of evolution than normal man, and he popularized the term "born criminal" to describe the lawbreaker who inherited his criminal tendencies either from criminal parents or from parents who had undergone a degenerative process. According to Lombroso, the born criminal exhibited physical and mental stigmata of his atavism. There were numerous stigmata, and they differed somewhat depending on the class of criminal (murderers, burglars, rapists, etc.), but among the most common were prognathism, square-headedness, and moral and physical insensitivity. ("Ne pas oublier les signes du criminel-né," Zola reminded himself in his notes for *La Bête*.)[58] Such characteristics, Lombroso believed, were the "outward and visible signs of a mysterious and complicated process of degeneration, which in the case of the criminal evokes evil impulses that are largely of atavistic origin."[59]

Lombroso's theories were popular in the late nineteenth century for several reasons. They not only confirmed superstitions about criminal physiognomy and about the effects of alcohol, but they also embodied an optimistic Darwinism, in which the criminal was a reversion to an earlier epoch rather than a product of evolutionary progress. Moreover, they supported the traditional belief in the "sins of the fathers," but did so by exact physical measurements and descriptions and by elaborate statistical proof. Zola was attracted to Lombroso's ideas because the entire Rougon-Macquart edifice was built on the foundation of hereditary alcoholic degeneracy; Norris because the idea of criminal atavism was a sensational endorsement of his ideas about the importance of man's animal past.

It is doubtful that Norris was aware of Lombroso's theories at first hand when he began writing *McTeague* in early 1895, despite the widespread knowledge of criminal anthropology at that time among both criminologists and laymen. Rather, the early influences in the novel appear to have been the Collins murder, *L'Assommoir*, and the characterization of Lantier in *La Bête humaine*. But by the time Norris completed *McTeague* in the fall of 1897, he had acquired and exhibited an acquaintance with Lombroso's ideas, though he had apparently still not read Lombroso at first hand. The most obvious source for this increase in knowledge is Max Nordau's *Degeneration*, which was published in March, 1895, and which by June had become the most discussed book of the year.[60] Nordau's study was dedicated to Lombroso and was an attempt to use the idea of the stigmata of degeneracy in an attack on the major artists and art movements of the day. Nordau not only mentioned Lombroso throughout his work, but also defined degeneracy in Lombrosian terms. "The degenerate organism," he wrote, "has not the power to mount to the height of evolution already attained by the species, but stops on the way."[61] Norris' story "A Case for Lombroso," which appeared in the *Wave* on September 11, 1897, reveals that he associated Lombroso with Nordau. He subtitled his clipping of the story, "A Subject for Max Nordau,"[62] and its theme is related to Nordau's depiction of egomania and morbidity among degenerate artists.

Norris may also have learned of Lombroso's ideas from his friend Dr. Lawlor, who from mid-1895 to mid-1898 was prison doctor at San Quentin.[63] Norris wrote two articles on San Quentin for the *Wave*, and in one of them, "New Year's at San Quentin" (January 9, 1897), he both accepted the idea of inherited homicidal mania and mentioned Dr. Lawlor by name.[64] Dr. Lawlor, as a prison doctor, would probably have known of Lombroso's theories, particularly at San Quentin, where the prison chaplin, August Drähms, was a confirmed Lombrosian, whose book *The Criminal* (1900) contained a commendatory preface by the master.[65]

That Norris during 1896-1897 was responding to the complex of ideas involving degeneracy and inherited criminality is revealed by a number of articles and stories which he wrote for the *Wave* during this period. One of his earliest *Wave* sketches, "Man Proposes—No. 2" (May 30, 1896), is about a coal heaver whose mother had "drunk herself into an asylum." He is a huge brute of a man, dull-witted and slow, with "his lower jaw immense, probably like the jaws of the carnivora."[66] (There is much in this sketch which is also in *McTeague*, but it is impossible to tell whether it draws upon the novel or vice versa.) In "A Reversion to Type" (August 14, 1897), a seemingly docile department store floorwalker suddenly reverts to the criminality of his father. "Little Dramas of the Curbstone" (June 26, 1897) combines the themes of alcoholic atavism and criminal reversion. The "dramas" are accounts of parental degeneracy which has resulted in children who are idiots, cripples, and criminals. Of one of the children, "a creature far below the brute," a medical student says, "Heredity . . . , father a degenerate, exhausted race, drank himself into a sanitarium." Norris concluded the sketch with the comment that "the chief actors [the fathers] in these three Little Dramas of the Curbstone had been somehow left out of the programme."[67]

These stories and sketches reveal Norris' preoccupation with the theme of atavism and reversion (the two terms were used interchangeably in his day), and particularly with the role of heredity in causing either an obvious physical or mental devolution or a return to an earlier family condition. Norris had dealt with the theme of reversion as early as 1891 in his story "The Son of a Sheik." It is a theme found frequently in Kipling, and indeed it appeared in much post-Darwinian literature once some of the implications of evolution were realized. ("Evolution ever climbing after some ideal good," Tennyson wrote, "and Reversion ever dragging evolution in the mud.") But in Norris' *Wave* pieces of 1896-1897, the theme appears in the context of alcoholism and criminality, which relates it significantly to Lombroso and *McTeague* rather than to Kipling.

Thus Norris' initial impulse to develop McTeague in terms of a brutish criminality caused by alcoholism was no doubt sharpened during the composition of the novel by the popularity of Nordau's and Lombroso's theories of degeneracy.[68] The result of this variety of influences impinging on the conception of McTeague is that though he is not a literal portrait of a Lombrosian born criminal, he does have sufficient characteristics of that type to indicate that Norris was loosely drawing upon contemporary ideas involving degeneracy and atavistic criminality. McTeague lacks many of the explicit stigmata listed by Lombroso, such as epilepsy and tattooing. McTeague's characteristics are rather those which indicate Norris' imaginative response to the dramatic possibilities inherent in the idea of alcoholic degeneracy resulting in atavistic criminality, particularly those characteristics which immediately suggest atavism, such as physical size and strength and mental slowness. So McTeague's father has died of acute alcoholism, and McTeague himself is huge, strong, stupid, and crude. Moreover, he has the protruding jaw,[69] square head, and alcoholic intolerance of the Lombrosian criminal.

McTeague is dull and slow except when roused to anger or desire, at which time the beast within him—"the brute that in McTeague lay so close to the surface" (VIII, 200)[70]—prompts him to seize or destroy with uncontrollable violence. Early in the novel he is a potential criminal when he kisses the anesthetized Trina and when he breaks Marcus' arm while wrestling. Later, under the influence of alcohol, which stimulates the release of a vicious brutality in him, he tortures and then murders Trina. After the murder, McTeague displays one of the outstanding characteristics of the atavistic criminal—lack of remorse for his crime. On his return to the Placer County mining area, he feels an instinctive kinship with the primeval landscape. Finally, in fleeing his pursuers, his persistence in traveling with his canary causes him to be easily followed, yet he possesses an animalistic sixth sense which warns him of approaching danger.

Responsive to the dramatic possibilities of the atavistic criminal and encouraged by Zola's many animal-like characters, Norris exaggerated McTeague into a gross brute of a man, just as he had exaggerated Vandover's sensuality into lycanthropic hallucinations. Not that the struggle between flesh and spirit does not occur within McTeague. As he views the anesthetized Trina,

> Suddenly the animal in the man stirred and woke; the evil instincts that in him were so close to the surface leaped to life, shouting and clamouring.
> . . . Within him, a certain second self, another better Mc-Teague rose with the brute; both were strong, with the huge crude strength of the man himself. . . . It was the old battle, old as the world, wide as the world—the sudden panther leap of the animal, lips drawn, fangs aflash, hideous, monstrous, not to be resisted, and the simultaneous arousing of the other man, the better self that cries, "Down, down," without knowing why; that grips the monster; that fights to strangle it, to thrust it down and back (VIII, 26).

In this first encounter with the "monster," however, McTeague succumbs immediately, as he crudely kisses Trina. Norris then asks the reason for this fall, and quickly answers his question:

> Why could he not always love her purely, cleanly? What was this perverse, vicious thing that lived within him, knitted to his flesh?
> Below the fine fabric of all that was good in him ran the foul stream of hereditary evil, like a sewer. The vices and sins of his father and of his father's father, to the third and fourth and five

hundredth generation, tainted him. The evil of an entire race flowed in his veins. Why should it be? He did not desire it. Was he to blame? (VIII, 27)

No wonder that Norris asks "Was he to blame?," for the implication is that, given McTeague's hereditary disposition toward atavism, the victory of the brute is beyond his control, though that victory—as all such victories—is to be deplored.

This notorious passage, blatant as it is, involves a more complex idea of McTeague's atavism than appears at first glance. For Norris' analysis of McTeague's "evil instincts" combines the limited theme of criminal atavism ("the vices and sins of his father") with the more generic theme of racial atavism—that is, the Le Contean theme of man's animal sensuality going back to the "five hundredth generation." Norris further develops this larger theme—or rather suggests more firmly its earlier presence—when he writes in the next paragraph that the pull of sexual desire had at last faced McTeague "as sooner or later it faces every child of man." His use of the term "race" in the passage also implies a dual atavistic theme. The term embodies both the common meaning of "mankind as a whole" and the more specialized sense of "family heritage." Norris had used it in this second sense in "Little Dramas of the Curbstone" and "A Case for Lombroso."[71] The passage is confusing because it rather muddily combines these two sources of McTeague's "foul stream of hereditary evil." But it is out of this complexity, here fuzzy but elsewhere clearer, that the main theme of the novel emerges. McTeague's fall is the product of both his special circumstance as an atavistic criminal and his general sensual fallibility as a man. Both flaws stress man's atavistic nature, that he is frequently controlled by unanalyzable instincts which derive from his family and racial past.

Norris, therefore, seems to have begun *McTeague* as a story of alcoholic degeneracy, closely related to this theme in Zola. He then saw the possibility of heightening his portrait of McTeague by introducing some of Lombroso's ideas on criminal atavism. But as he filled out and rewrote the novel, he probably realized that the theme of atavism involved more than an explanation of the criminal, that it also embodied other central human characteristics which absorbed him, that most of all it was related to the source and nature of man's sexual desires. Under the impact of this larger conception of atavism, Norris expanded and developed the novel in directions either absent or barely implied in his original plan. He now gave more attention to the courtship and marriage of Trina and McTeague than to Trina's murder or McTeague's capture; he introduced two additional love subplots; and he made Trina's avarice a parallel atavistic theme to McTeague's criminality. And it is this expansion of the atavistic theme, until it transcends Norris' source of it in the Collins murder and in Zola and Lombroso, which almost succeeds in turning the novel into that mythical creature of literature, a naturalistic tragedy.

6

McTeague has two main divisions. The first contains the courtship and wedding of Trina and McTeague and the generally happy and placid first five years of their marriage. It ends with McTeague's loss of his occupation. The second is devoted to their decline, until Trina is murdered and McTeague is left handcuffed to the dead Marcus in the desert. (In addition, each division has two segments. The first breaks neatly at the wedding feast into courtship and marriage, the second at Trina's murder into the couple's decline and the pursuit of McTeague.) One way to analyze the novel is to show how the various themes, plots, and symbols introduced in the first half of the work come to fruition in the second.

McTeague and Trina exhibit characteristics in the first division of the novel which later contribute to their downfall. They do not fall because of one overriding flaw in themselves or their world, but because of the interrelated action of a number of causes. Norris, however, stresses one generic force which in its various forms is a primary cause of their decline—the uncontrollable power of the past. His theme is that man's racial atavism (particularly his sexual desires) and man's individual family heritage combine as a force toward reversion—that is, toward a return to the emotions and instincts of his animal past—which under propitious circumstances controls and dominates him. The fatalism inherent in this theme encouraged Norris to introduce chance as another major factor in men's lives. Here he was probably also influenced by Zola's striking use of chance in *L'Assommoir*, in which Coupeau's accidental fall from a roof plays such an important role. Yet, like Zola, and indeed like Shakespeare as well, Norris so intertwines chance, action, and character that the effect is of the complexity of experience rather than of the dominant role of fate.

The relationship between Trina and McTeague exhibits this complexity while stressing the role of the past. Their courtship, culminating in the marriage feast, occupies the first nine chapters of the novel. During this period of about six months they have three major encounters. The first, when McTeague kisses Trina in the dental chair, has already been discussed. It introduces McTeague's atavistic brutality, stemming from his racial and family past. When Trina awakens, McTeague clumsily proposes. Trina rejects him, "suddenly seized with a fear of him, the intuitive feminine fear of the male" (VIII, 28). At this point in their courtship, Norris is at pains to stress the overt sexual innocence yet intuitive racial sexuality of both Trina and McTeague. The woman in Trina "was not yet awakened; she was yet, as one might say, without sex. She was almost like a boy, frank, candid, unreserved" (VIII, 20). For McTeague, Trina is his "first experience. With her the feminine element suddenly entered his little world. It was not only her that he saw or felt, it was the woman, the whole sex, an entire new humanity, strange and alluring, that he seemed to have discovered" (VIII, 23). Despite this innocence and lack of experience, both react along intuitive racial lines—McTeague desiring to seize and possess her, she instinctively withdrawing, yet—as we shall see—desiring to be conquered. At this point it is McTeague in particular who is helpless in the grip of his desire. " 'It's something that's just stronger than you are,' " he explains to Marcus. " 'I was so close to her I touched her face every minute, and her mouth, and smelt her hair and her breath . . .' " (VIII, 47).

The second and most important sexual encounter between McTeague and Trina occurs at the B Street Station, where McTeague again proposes. When Trina hesitates, he seizes her "in his enormous arms, crushing down her struggle with his immense strength. Then Trina gave up, all in an instant, turning her head to his. They kissed each other, grossly, full on the mouth" (VIII, 72). Within the literary conventions of the day, this kiss symbolizes Trina's sexual submission. At this moment, therefore, another strand in the web of sexual determinism begins to pull taut, for "the instant that Trina gave up, the instant she allowed him to kiss her, he thought less of her. She was not so desirable, after all." McTeague senses this diminution along with a vague awareness "that this must be so, that it belonged to the changeless order of things—the man desiring the woman only for what she withholds; the woman worshipping the man for that which she yields up to him. With each concession gained the man's

65

desire cools; with every surrender made the woman's adoration increases. But why should it be so?" (VIII, 73). Norris in this second meeting is concerned not with a particular weakness in McTeague or Trina, but with a sexual determinism affecting all men.

This theme continues into the next chapter, which opens with an analysis of Trina's feelings toward McTeague. She recognizes that she has responded primarily to his brute strength, and she feels a kind of "necessity" in that reaction. "Why," she asks herself,

> did she feel the desire, the necessity of being conquered by a superior strength? Why did it please her? Why had it suddenly thrilled her from head to foot with a quick terrifying gust of passion, the like of which she had never known. . . ?
>
> When McTeague had all at once caught her in his huge arms, something had leaped to life in her—something that had hitherto lain dormant, something strong and overpowering. It frightened her now as she thought of it, this second self that had wakened within her, and that shouted and clamoured for recognition (VIII, 76-77).

This "second self" or awakened Woman—Norris' euphemisms for sexual desire—is not evil. Trina "knew she was a pure girl; knew that this sudden commotion within her carried with it no suggestion of vice" (VIII, 77). Yet, once aroused, it is an uncontrollable, unselective emotion.

> Did she choose him for better or for worse, deliberately, of her own free will, or was Trina herself allowed even a choice in the taking of that step that was to make or mar her life? The Woman is awakened, and, starting from her sleep, catches blindly at what first her newly opened eyes light upon. It is a spell, a witchery, ruled by chance alone, inexplicable—a fairy queen enamoured of a clown with ass's ears (VIII, 77).

The possessive sexual desire of the man aroused by the first woman he experiences sensually, the instinctive desire of the

66

woman for sexual submission responding to the first man who assaults her—these are the atavistic animal forces which bring Trina and McTeague together. Norris concludes by stating that "Their undoing had already begun. Yet neither of them was to blame. From the first they had not sought each other. Chance had brought them face to face, and mysterious instincts as ungovernable as the winds of heaven were at work knitting their lives together" (VIII, 78). Norris' point is that man's racial sexual nature, not individual conscious choice, is the prime factor in interweaving two lives. He exaggerated the role of this factor in *McTeague* because his couple are intellectually and sexually naive. (Trina, too, finds that it is "quite beyond her" to understand her feelings [VIII, 77].) But even when Norris in later works dealt with more sophisticated couples, he still tended to see courtship and marriage more as a product of large racial forces than of individual choice.

The third sexual meeting between Trina and McTeague occurs after their wedding feast, and is a short, emphatic restatement of their relationship. Trina is again afraid, but "an immense joy seized upon [McTeague]—the joy of possession. . . . Those instincts that in him were so close to the surface suddenly leaped to life, shouting and clamouring, not to be resisted." Again he crushes her in his arms, "kissing her full upon the mouth. Then her great love for McTeague suddenly flashed up in Trina's breast; she gave up to him as she had done before, yielding all at once to that strange desire of being conquered and subdued" (VIII, 155).

The question remains, why does this courtship and marriage bring about their "undoing"? It does so because their sexual attraction has led them into a match which causes their eventual destruction when other forces in their characters and world begin to operate. The almost entirely physical nature of McTeague's love for Trina is clear enough, and is demonstrated further by the quick fading of his love after marriage, considerably before they begin having difficulties. Trina's sexuality is less obvious, for she is a "good girl" who continues to love McTeague for many years after their marriage. But her love, Norris frequently stated, is based almost entirely on McTeague's conquest and her surrender. Norris also gives Trina a distinctive symbol of sexuality, a rich crown of black hair. This was as familiar a symbol of sensuality in the nineteenth century as large breasts in the twentieth, and was often so used by Zola. One of Norris' early descriptions of Trina's hair suggests her self-devouring sensuality, a suggestion borne out later in the novel:

> The dentist saw her again, as if for the first time, her small, pale face looking out from beneath her royal tiara of black hair; he saw again her long, narrow blue eyes; her lips, nose, and tiny ears, pale and bloodless, and suggestive of anaemia, as if all the vitality that should have lent them colour had been sucked up into the strands and coils of that wonderful hair (VIII, 139).

Norris introduced into the courtship of Trina by McTeague key symbolic acts and settings which reflect the underlying flaws in their relationship despite their exhilaration and joy. Trina vomits after McTeague's proposal in the dental parlor; the B Street Station is a bleak wasteland, and the kiss between Trina and McTeague is interrupted by a roaring train; and the wedding feast is a gross stuffing. Although the courtship appears to reach a successful and happy conclusion in marriage, the theme of "undoing" is justified by Norris' portrayal of the unselective sexual desire which has joined the fairy queen and the clown.

The second part of the first half of the novel, that devoted to the marriage until McTeague's loss of his profession, is concerned primarily with McTeague's and Trina's personal rather than racial atavistic flaws. And just as the theme of racial atavism had included the theme of chance, so chance here too plays a major role.

Trina wins a $5,000 lottery prize, which activates her hereditary avarice and encourages Marcus' jealousy of McTeague. Marcus had at first enjoyed his generosity in giving up Trina to Mc-Teague, but after Trina's stroke of luck his quarrelsome nature and quickness of temper lead him to believe that he has been wronged, and eventually he informs the authorities that McTeague is practicing without a diploma. McTeague therefore loses his profession because of the interaction between chance and a particular temperament, an interaction which exemplifies Norris' treatment of the theme of chance.

Trina's miserliness appears after her marriage, when for the first time she manages a household and also has the impetus to save given her by the $5,000. Her niggardliness is atavistic in two senses. First, it is a "reversion to type." Trina is of Swiss-German stock: "a good deal of peasant blood still ran undiluted in her veins, and she had all the instincts of a hardy and penurious mountain race—the instinct which saves without any thought, without idea of consequence—saving for the sake of saving, hoarding without knowing why" (VIII, 116-17). Secondly, the instinct is uncontrollable. " 'It's stronger than I,' " Trina says. " 'It's growing on me, but never mind, it's a good fault, and, anyhow, I can't help it' " (VIII, 180). An incident toward the end of the first half of the novel anticipates the power of this instinct to drive out all other emotions. When Trina's parents write to her for money, she sends only McTeague's share and then lies to him about how much she has sent—acts in which love of money is stronger than love of husband and parents.

After McTeague can no longer practice, these two atavistic characteristics of Trina—one not vice, the other "a good thing"—become abnormal under the pressure of events. McTeague turns brutal toward her, and her earlier desire to be conquered becomes an abnormal masochism. McTeague bites her fingers and beats her, "and in some strange, inexplicable way this brutality made Trina all the more affectionate; aroused in her a morbid, unwholesome love of submission, a strange, unnatural pleasure in yielding, in surrendering herself to the will of an irresistible, virile power" (VIII, 263). As money becomes more difficult to acquire and keep, her earlier miserliness becomes avarice. Gradually, her love of money and her sexual nature begin to merge in a union which underlines both the intensity of these emotions and their instinctive, atavistic source. She plays sensuously with her gold coins, putting "her small fingers into the pile with little murmurs of affection, her long, narrow eyes half closed and shining, her breath coming in long sighs" (VIII, 262). Her emotions are now but two, "her passion for her money and her perverted love for her husband when he was brutal" (VIII, 263-64). At last, her love for McTeague is destroyed when he steals the $400 which she has hidden in her trunk, and her love for money becomes even more explicitly sexual. Her desire for gold is now "a mania, a veritable mental disease" (VIII, 303), and she draws out all of her $5,000 in gold coins. "One evening she had even spread all the gold pieces between the sheets, and had then gone to bed, stripping herself, and had slept all night upon the money, taking a strange and ecstatic pleasure in the touch of the smooth flat pieces the length of her entire body" (VIII, 306). At this point, with her instinctive avarice and sensuality united and uncontrollably powerful, she is as much a "brute" in the context of her own nature and sex as is the McTeague who shortly after murders her.

The same process of degeneration to excessive brutality occurs in McTeague. His brute sensuality becomes dormant after his marriage, but it is replaced by another aspect of his animal nature, his ferocity when angered or when drinking. Like Trina's avarice, this characteristic emerges clearly after their marriage and then dominates him once he loses his profession. It appears first in the scene in which Marcus breaks McTeague's pipe, and it is fully developed during their wrestling match, after Marcus bites McTeague's ear. With the spilling of blood, there

> followed a terrible scene. The brute that in McTeague lay so close to the surface leaped instantly to life, monstrous, not to be resisted. He sprang to his feet with a shrill and meaningless clamour, totally unlike the ordinary bass of his speaking tones. It was the hideous yelling of a hurt beast. . . . It was something no longer human; it was rather an echo from the jungle.
>
> Sluggish enough and slow to anger on ordinary occasions, McTeague when finally aroused became another man. His rage was a kind of obsession, an evil mania, the drunkenness of passion, the exalted and perverted fury of the Berserker, blind and deaf, a thing insensate (VIII, 200-201).

In the second half of the novel, McTeague's atavistic ferocity—that aspect of his character closest to Norris' idea of the Lombrosian criminal—emerges as his dominant characteristic. Like Trina's flaws, its growth is encouraged by external circumstances. Out of a job, embittered by Trina's miserliness, unhappy in their tiny room, disturbed by the loss of pride, stability, and order which his profession gave him, tempted by the convivial tippling of Polk Street, McTeague begins to drink. Alcohol does not make him drunk, but "roused the man, or rather the brute in the man, and now not only roused it, but goaded it to evil" (VIII, 261). His annoyance at Trina's avarice turns to savagery when he drinks, and at last, after drinking all day, he murders her.

Of course, in this analysis of Trina and McTeague, I have simplified both characters, and particularly McTeague. I have said little or nothing about his love of order and routine, his relation to his profession, or his pride—all of which contribute to his fullness as a character and to our response to his fall. I will take these up in other contexts. Rather, I have attempted to describe

71

the core characteristics of McTeague and Trina, and therefore the central theme of the novel.

A major part of this central theme involves the sexual tragedy of man and woman. Caught up by drives and instincts beyond their control or comprehension, they mate by chance rather than by will. This theme dominates the first half of the novel. But Norris backs away from a full exploration of this complex and moving idea by combining it with the theme of the atavistic criminal. The novel was begun as a sensational story of a degenerate alcoholic brute, and much of its origin remains in the physical depiction of McTeague, in the early scene with Trina in the dental parlor, and in the later scenes of McTeague's drunken brutality. But as Norris worked toward the denouement which had originally attracted him to the story, he responded to the theme of a sexual determinism deriving from man's animal nature. In *McTeague*, sex is not simply a step toward degeneration, as it is in *Vandover*. It is rather that which comes to all men and women, disrupting their lives and placing them in relationships which the sanctity of marriage cannot prevent from ending in chaos and destruction.

Both novels deal with the "brute" in man. And though *Vandover* embodies a more traditional idea of free will and responsibility, *McTeague* is ultimately the more compelling treatment of man's sexual nature. It does not tell the old tale of the fallen fornicator, but reaches out toward the unexplored ground of the human dilemma of sexual attraction. But though it reaches out, it does not really seize, for welded to the theme of sexual fatalism and atavism is the theme of the Lombrosian criminal. The two themes are joined "intellectually," one might say, because both stress the power of man's biological inheritance, whether racial or familial. But "dramatically" they are less successfully joined, since the theme of McTeague as a human being

72

caught up in the web of sex and chance is at least partially vitiated by his extraordinariness as a brute criminal.

7

The two subplots play various roles in the novel, with that of the Maria-Zerkow subplot the most obvious. A rather static plot, its only forward movement is the marriage of the pair (announced rather than presented), Maria's amnesia, Zerkow's murder of Maria, and his own death. It begins with both characters in an advanced state of degeneracy: the half-crazed Mexican with a "diseased imagination," the preternaturally avaricious Jewish junk man. Most of its action consists of Zerkow's absorption in Maria's story of the gold plate, until he believes in its reality and murders her because he thinks she is hiding it from him. The subplot thus anticipates Trina's gold mania, which also ends in murder. Less obvious is the connection between Norris' choice of characters for this subplot and the central theme of the main plot. Zerkow is a Jew, Maria of Latin blood, and Norris characterizes them along racial lines. (Norris' Chinese are crafty, his Latins hot-blooded, his Jews miserly, his Anglo-Saxons adventurous, and so on.)[72] Zerkow's avarice is as much a racial "reversion to type" as is Trina's. The subplot therefore reinforces the main plot not only by foreshadowing the tragic effects of avarice, but also by reintroducing the theme of the racial source of that flaw.

Although the thematic relationship of the Zerkow-Maria story to the main plot is strident and contrived, the account of their fall engenders a force of its own. Maria's repeated sensuous narratives of her family's gold plate eventually achieve a ritualistic intensity, and we become involved in Zerkow's fascination with her story and in the possible effects of that fascination. There is little, however, to be said for the Old Grannis-Miss Baker sub-

73

plot, the third of the novel's three love stories. It is a foil to the two disastrous love stories. Instead of passion, greed, and brutality, Old Grannis and Miss Baker's affair contains shyness, kindness, and gentleness—the last two particularly in the climactic scene in which Miss Baker offers Old Grannis a cup of tea. Also, as William B. Dillingham persuasively argues, they are finally brought together by the same forces of chance and instinct which govern the main plot.[73] Yet the Old Grannis-Miss Baker subplot is thematically and dramatically weak. First, they are an elderly couple with many of the distinctive characteristics of the old. Their shyness derives primarily from "the timidity of their second childhood" (VIII, 149), and their love is asexual. They are two lonely old people who come together, with little suggestion of any sexual response to each other. Because their subplot contains the only successful love match in the novel, Norris seems to be saying that love must be asexual if it is to have the virtues of restraint, generosity, and kindness, and if it is to end in happiness. This suggestion is irrelevant to the sexual theme in the main plot (the sexual dilemma "faces every child of man"), and it is false to Norris' treatment elsewhere of the role of sexual attraction in happy and successful marriages—most notably in his popular novels and in *The Octopus*. Secondly, the old couple are simply boring. Their "affair" is even more static than Zerkow's and Maria's, and it lacks the intensity of that relationship. Their shyness controls all their actions, and in this sense they are Dickensian characters, as many critics have noted. They fail not because they are Dickensian but because they are weakly Dickensian— because their "humour" is neither inherently rich nor vigorously portrayed and therefore cannot bear repetition.

The three love stories, each dominated by a central emotion (passion, greed, shyness), provide a major unifying force in the novel. Two other unifying devices are the gold symbolism and the

Polk Street setting. The gold symbolism has often been attacked.[74] No doubt it is obsessively present and is occasionally
forced, as when Trina believes that the sunlight in her room falls
into a pattern of gold coins. But its ubiquitousness is defensible
when one realizes that gold is not simply a symbol for greed—
though that is its most striking use—but also for anything of
value. Gold symbolizes what a particular character desires or
values, and that may be money or it may be something else. Norris is not muddled when he has Trina desire gold coins, but has
McTeague desire a sign in the shape of a gold tooth; he is rather
transferring gold from a universal symbol of wealth to a personal
symbol of value, as is common in everyday usage.

The dominant gold symbolism, of course, is that of avarice in
relation to Trina and Zerkow. Its use here involves more than appears on the surface, for Norris not only symbolized avarice by
the desire for gold, but associated the desire for the physical
reality of the metal with primitive longings. In a *Wave* article
(July 31, 1897) on the sailing of an Alaskan gold rush ship, Norris wrote: "One hasn't got so far beyond the primitive type, after
all—at least, not so far but that the first touch of gold, the pure,
crude, virgin metal, stirs us to a ferment of emotion, a very fever
heat of cupidity and desire."[75] The lust of Trina and Zerkow for
the physical metal, and their sensual response to it, reinforces the
theme of the atavistic, racial source of their avarice. When Trina
fondles her gold coins, or when Zerkow's fingers twitch at the
sight of gold, Norris is uniting avarice and atavism in one symbol.

Gold is again symbolically associated with the primitive in the
last section of the novel, when McTeague returns to the Placer
County gold mining area of his youth. Norris works hard in this
section to project an aura of the primitive and animal-like, stressing particularly the rough, untamed countryside. Nature in Placer
County is not "cosy, intimate, small, and homelike," but is "a

vast, unconquered brute of the Pliocene epoch, savage, sullen, and magnificently indifferent to man" (VIII, 322). McTeague's instinctive return to this area is like a hunted animal's return to its lair, and his reliance on an intuitive sixth sense to avoid capture intensifies this theme. His gold mining activities in this section are therefore more closely allied to the theme of his animal nature than to a theme of greed. Indeed, Norris links gold and the primitive directly when he has McTeague lead an animal-like existence at the Big Dipper Mine, working at night in the bowels of the earth and sleeping by day.

The second major use of the gold symbolism is as a personal symbol of value for McTeague. Throughout the novel he is constantly involved with the metal. He works on his gold dental mats, longs for a gold tooth sign, and owns a canary in a gilt cage. Later, he steals Trina's gold, discovers gold while mining, and finally kills Marcus in a fight over Trina's gold coins. The gold tooth is one of the major symbols in the novel. Before his marriage McTeague yearns for the sign. It represents his pride in his profession, and in a large sense it symbolizes for him the dental profession as a whole. Norris carefully documents McTeague's life as a dentist. He does so not simply for verisimilitude, but because McTeague's occupation is at the center of his life. Its habitual tasks and minor successes represent the order and stability which McTeague requires, given his limited intelligence, if his life is to have any meaning and if it is not to disintegrate into the brutality which, in Norris' oft-repeated words, is in McTeague so close to the surface. The gold tooth is therefore McTeague's sign to the world and to himself of his pride in his profession and of its importance in his life. It is one of the major ironies of the novel—somewhat like his later discovery of gold—that Trina should buy the tooth for him as a birthday present just before their marriage.

McTeague's canary in its gilt cage and his concertina are also symbols of the role of order and routine in his life. They represent the commonplace, repetitive pleasures of his daily existence. When McTeague loses his profession, he attempts to cling to these symbols of pride and order as a kind of recompense for the loss of the actuality. He refuses to part with the tooth, and he stubbornly holds the canary and the concertina back from the auction.

Norris parallels the importance of the gold tooth in McTeague's life and gold in Trina's by passages in which each character's response to his central symbol is couched in religious imagery. On the night that McTeague receives the Tooth (Norris' capital), he wakes often to look at it, and each time senses it as "a huge, vague bulk, looming there through the half darkness in the centre of the room, shining dimly out as if with some mysterious light of its own" (VIII, 130). For Trina, the lottery prize becomes "a thing miraculous, a god-from-the-machine, suddenly descending upon the stage of her humble little life; she regarded it as something almost sacred and inviolable" (VIII, 134). Both the tooth and the prize are gods to those worshiping them. When McTeague finally sells the tooth to the "Other Dentist," it is an act signifying the loss of the last vestiges of moral order given to his life by his profession. The canary and the concertina persist longer as symbols of his old life. He is incensed when he discovers that Trina has sold his concertina, and his anger plays a role in her murder. The canary he keeps till the end—a last symbol of the narrow but ordered world which he has lost but which he still dimly desires.

It is this characteristic of McTeague, that of the circumscribed intelligence deprived of its world of meaning and pride, which, along with the theme of sexual determinism, raises his portrayal above that of a degenerate criminal and makes him a sympathetic

77

character. He is a huge, dull man, slow to recognize insult, but he doesn't like to be "made small of." When he thinks a theatre ticket clerk is chaffing him, or when the "Other Dentist" offers to buy his tooth, or when Trina refuses him carfare, his limited understanding and pride are offended, and he replies with an angry " 'You can't make small of me.' " His murder of Trina, therefore, is more than an outburst of drunken atavistic ferocity, though this element is present. He murders her partly because he is affronted by her refusal to aid him when he was starving and by her sale of his concertina. He wants her $5,000 as revenge for her plaguing avarice and as a means of salvaging his self-respect. " 'You ain't going to make small of me this time,' " he tells her just before striking the first blow (VIII, 318). McTeague's final struggle with Marcus is on a similar basis. They fight not for the gold itself, since they both recognize that they are stranded in the desert, but because each feels that he has been wronged by the other and that pride and the redress of wrong require the possession of Trina's gold.

Our changing emotional response to McTeague and Trina results partly from this dimension in McTeague's character and partly from Norris' awkward combination of racial and familial atavistic themes. Trina is at first sympathetic as a confused and troubled young girl, but she later loses our sympathy because of her avarice, and becomes primarily a curiosity. We never fully identify ourselves with McTeague in the early parts of the novel. Although, like Trina, he is troubled, he is too dull and brutish. But in the second half we begin to feel compassion for him as he becomes a victim of Trina's avarice and as we recognize that his emerging brutality is at least partly the result of the destruction of his world. Our emotions cross late in the first half of the novel, when McTeague learns that he can no longer practice dentistry. Trina's concern in this event is primarily monetary, but Mc-

Teague feels that he has lost all meaning in life. In a scene of some power Trina comes upon him sitting in his dental chair, "looking stupidly out of the window, across the roofs opposite, with an unseeing gaze, his red hands lying idly in his lap" (VIII, 229). We are never completely one with McTeague, of course. His brute strength and dull mind put us off. But because he is trapped in the universal net of sex, and because we recognize the poignancy of his desire not to be made small of—particularly once his profession is lost—we respond to him ultimately as a human being in distress rather than as an anomaly.

The last major source of unity in *McTeague* is its Polk Street setting. Norris subtitled the novel "A Story of San Francisco" and once thought of calling it "The People of Polk Street."[76] ("The Golden Tooth" was yet another tentative title.)[77] The life of Polk Street enters the novel in two ways—through set pieces describing either street activities or the daily lives of the central characters in relation to the life of the street, and through constant incidental allusion to its activities and inhabitants. As in *Vandover*, Norris creates a world of concrete actuality to lend a sense of the possible to the sensational events of the plot. But Polk Street serves an additional major function in *McTeague*. Norris' descriptions dramatically establish it as above all a life of the repetitive and constant. It therefore creates a texture of the ordered and routine in McTeague's life, of a world where the harness shop, the grocery, and the car conductors' coffee joint are always available in their set roles, where the children go to school at the same time each morning, to be followed by the shop clerks coming to work, and so on. McTeague is settled and content in this life, and we recognize that his inner needs and outer world are in harmony.

Norris is equally effective in handling another part of McTeague's Polk Street world, his rooming house (or flat, as Norris calls it). Just as he perhaps derived the idea of a repetitive street world from *L'Assommoir*, so he borrowed Zola's technique in that novel of grouping many of his central characters in a large tenement building. He goes beyond Zola, however, by centering all his plots in the flat. Of the seven principal characters in *McTeague*, five live in the building when the novel opens, Trina soon moves in, and Zerkow lives just behind it. This device allows Norris to interweave his plots efficiently, often bringing them together in key scenes, such as the lottery ticket purchase or the wedding feast. It allows him also to establish symbolic physical moves or symbolic shifts in relationship, as when Trina and McTeague move into Zerkow's room after Maria's murder, or as when Trina neglects the friendship of Miss Baker for that of Maria.

Norris, in fact, creates four levels or circles of concrete reality, each connected with the others in plot or theme, and each expressed with such expert control of repetitive detail that almost all the physical reality of the novel is open to symbolic interpretation. First, there is the world of McTeague's dental parlor—his lovingly arranged room with its symbols of his pride in his profession and of his intellectual limitations. Then there are the worlds of the flat and of Polk Street. Finally, there is the widest circle, the world of San Francisco, and particularly the lower middle-class world of Sunday picnics, evenings at the vaudeville, and window shopping on Market Street. Each of these worlds is rendered with a detail and repetitiousness which suggest the commonplace and unexceptional. Yet each, in accord with Norris' belief that the romance of the extraordinary can be found "in the brownstone house on the corner and in the office building downtown,"[78] has its sensational moment. It is as though the initial paradox of a murder in a kindergarten were the stimulus for such scenes as McTeague kissing the anesthetized Trina in his dental parlor or the near-murderous fight between Marcus and McTeague at the picnic. Some of the best moments in the novel unite these two streams of the commonplace and the extraordinary with great power. One such moment is when the frightened and incoherent Trina, having just found Maria's corpse with its cut throat and its blood-soaked clothes, rushes out into the commonplace and everyday routine of Polk Street, and has difficulty convincing the butcher's boy that something is wrong or herself that it is not improper "to make a disturbance and create a scene in the street" (VIII, 269). The four circles of actuality also exist in what might be called a temporal density, which makes their details particularly susceptible to symbolic use. For example, on the night that Trina is robbed and deserted by McTeague, she wanders along Polk Street, hoping to find him. For one moment she rests on the horse block in front of their flat and recalls that she stood there when getting out of her carriage on her wedding day. *McTeague* is "A Story of San Francisco" not because its characters are "local types," but because San Francisco is inseparable from the current and form of their lives.

The three concluding chapters of *McTeague*, which narrate McTeague's adventures after Trina's murder, have often been criticized as melodramatic and anticlimactic. The section, however, has several functions in relation to the rest of the novel. As I have noted, it effectively reinforces the atavism theme. Having committed a brutal murder, McTeague instinctively returns to the occupation and to the primitive scenes of his youth. The three chapters, in short, involve the hunting of an animal-like criminal in a primitive setting after a bestial murder. In these chapters the outer expression of "the brute that in [McTeague] slept so close to the surface" is his sixth sense rather than sexual desire or animal ferocity, its earlier manifestations. Its reappearance even in this guise links the closing section firmly with the rest of the novel. Moreover, the novel comes full circle structurally with these last three chapters. It began with McTeague, then widened to include the three plots. After chapter XVII, it narrowed to McTeague and Trina, but finally, following Trina's death, it returns to McTeague alone.

To most readers, however, the effect of the last three chapters is less that of thematic or structural relevance than of narrative adventure. We are involved most of all in a good melodramatic chase, with McTeague's sixth sense more interesting as a narrative device which allows him to keep one jump ahead of his pursuers than as a thematic link. There are a number of glaring errors in plot, plausibility, and fact in this section. Norris suddenly shifts from December to May; he broadens Death Valley to over three times its width; and few canaries could survive the hegira McTeague's bird experiences. Moreover, in a novel which contains a rich supply of diseased and neurotic minds, it is perhaps too much to have McTeague's mule go mad from loco weed in the last chapter. Yet ultimately these are all quibbles. The close of *McTeague* is melodrama, but it is effective melodrama convincingly related to the rest of the novel.

In general, *McTeague* has fewer stylistic flaws than *Vandover*. Except for some notable lapses, Norris maintained a greater objectivity toward his material in *McTeague*, coloring fewer passages with morally loaded symbols or imagery. It has sometimes been argued that this greater control results from the difference in social status between the two protagonists, that Norris could be more objective about his lower-class dentist than about his middle-class artist because he felt aloof from the first but was emotionally involved with the second. The presence of some morally subjective passages in *McTeague*, however, indicates that Norris was to some extent personally involved in his characters' lives, and that the greater authorial detachment in *McTeague* is probably the result of greater artistic control. The most important of these passages of authorial presence in *McTeague* is Norris' analysis of McTeague's conflict when Trina is anesthetized. A good deal of nonsense has been written about this passage, accusing Norris of sexual infantilism and galloping Victorianism. His analysis is execrable, but not because of its theme that McTeague has committeed a despicable overt sexual act—the kiss, "grossly, full on the mouth"—against a helpless patient. If the situation were transferred to a modern novel and became a scene in which a man rapes a drunken girl at a party there would be no outcry against it or against the depiction of it as contemptible. Its weakness, rather, is that of so many passages in *Vandover*, of Norris' inability to escape moral absolutes and images reflecting those absolutes when he attempted interior analysis. Later in the courtship, when McTeague is alone in Trina's room and impulsively gathers her clothes in his arms and savors their odor, we have a striking and successful dramatization of the same theme of sexual desire.

Two other weaknesses of style or tone might be noted. One is Norris' occasional condescension toward the social status and habits of his characters, as when he writes of McTeague's "sham education and plebeian tastes" (VIII, 24). For the most part, however, he successfully captures the flavor of that education and taste in his accounts of McTeague's typical Sunday afternoons or of a wonderful courting conversation between Trina and McTeague. She tells him of a cousin who drowned in the bay and he counters with a car-boy bitten by a rattlesnake. (" 'He was a Frenchman, named Andrew. He swelled up and began to twitch' " [VIII, 59].) The second stylistic weakness is the rather heavyhanded satire of middle-class German immigrant life in the Sieppis. Norris caricatures them, and their frequent appearance early in the novel tends to distract from the tragic possibilities of the relationship between Trina and McTeague.

For *McTeague* is in part a tragic novel. True, McTeague neither bears full responsibility for his fall nor is he in any sense noble or profound. He is rather like Gervaise in *L'Assommoir:* they are both poor creatures who want above all a place to rest and be content yet who are brought low by their needs and desires. There is a sense of common humanity about McTeague's fall, despite his grotesqueness, and that quality is perhaps the modern residue of the tragic theme, since we are no longer so certain of man's transcendent nobility or of the reality of total responsibility for our fates. The theme of *McTeague* is not that greed and drunkenness lead to a tragic fall, but that tragedy is inherent in the human situation given man's animal past and the possibility that he will be dominated by that past in particular circumstances. At the point in the novel when McTeague has escaped to the mountains, Norris writes of the sounds of nature:

> Then one could hear the noises that the mountains made in their living. From the cañon, from the crowding crests, from the whole immense landscape, there rose a steady and prolonged sound, coming from all sides at once. It was that incessant and muffled roar which disengages itself from all vast bodies, from oceans, from cities, from forests, from sleeping armies, and which is like the breathing of an infinitely great monster, alive, palpitating (VIII, 329).

This image of life as an immense monster also appears in *Vandover*, when Norris describes San Francisco at night:

> All the lesser staccato noises of the day had long since died to silence; there only remained that prolonged and sullen diapason, coming from all quarters at once. It was like the breathing of some infinitely great monster, alive and palpitating, the systole and diastole of some gigantic heart (V, 202).

Vandover and the Brute AND McTeague

The image is an appropriate one for the two novels. It suggests that in *Vandover* and *McTeague* Norris was above all concerned with life's animal forces and with the tragic possibilities of the destructive emotions and instincts present in those forces.

Chapter Three

Moran of the Lady Letty, Blix,
AND A Man's Woman

1

Norris' three popular novels have usually been ignored or casually dismissed because of their obvious defects. Most critics agree that *Moran* is absurd, *Blix* slight, and A *Man's Woman* tedious. Like the lesser efforts of many writers, however, the three novels shed light on Norris' more complex and successful work and on his basic cast of mind. Moreover, despite their admitted weaknesses, they occasionally exhibit flashes of Norris at his best.

Moran, Blix, and A *Man's Woman* are written within popular formulas. All appeared originally in newspapers and magazines, and all are love stories set in the conventional molds of the novel of adventure, of courtship, and of exploration. They were written at a time when Norris was anxious for recognition and success, and they follow the recipe of adventure and love in exotic settings reestablished in the 1890's by such writers as Kipling, Stevenson, and Davis. (*Blix* seems to be somewhat outside this pattern, but is not, as we shall see.) Norris had often used this formula in his short stories, and in 1898 he began to apply it to the novel.

Moran of the Lady Letty, Blix, AND *A Man's Woman*

It may seem, at first glance, that Norris' popular fiction lies out-side his central themes and ideas, since it bears little immediate resemblance to his more important work. Norris' idea of man's ethical duality, however, involved not only the belief that man's animal heritage might lead him to disaster, but also that this same animal past might supply man with the force necessary to strengthen his moral courage and his will to achieve. But man could seldom gain the full benefit of this part of his animal nature, Norris believed, without the aid of a strong woman, who by her own firmness of will called forth this quality in man. This idea of the correct use of man's animal nature is easily absorbed into the conventions of popular fiction with their emphasis on a vigorous hero and a love story. Norris in his popular novels, there-fore, does not simply imitate a successful formula, but reshapes that formula—occasionally with surprising results—into a vehicle for his particular moral view of love and adventure.

In one of his earliest short stories, "The Way of the World" (July 26, 1892), Norris stated his belief in the crucial role of women in man's development—that "whatever is the station of the woman relative to that of the man, she will bring him down to her level long before he can lift her to his—if hers be the higher, she will raise him to it; if it be lower, though by ever so little, she will bring him down to it."[1] This conventional nine-teenth-century idea, however, was only a base on which Norris constructed an elaborate, and sometimes distinctive, masculine-feminine ethic. The major source of this elaboration was Le Conte's dualism with its beneficial role for man's "more robust" lower nature in nourishing and strengthening his higher faculties. It was woman's task, Norris believed, to aid the development of this aspect of man's animal nature by herself embodying a strength and seriousness of purpose—for her to implicitly sug-gest a masculine force and robustness, for her to be, in short, what Norris called a "man's woman." In this conception of the serious-minded woman and her role, Norris was influenced by the work of Charles Dana Gibson, and indeed his first use of the term "man's woman" occurs in a review of Gibson's drawings in December, 1896. A Gibson girl, Norris wrote,

> is very tall and a little slim, and her dignity and imposing carriage are her great characteristics. She is rather grave, doesn't smile often, and then mostly with the eyes. Nor is she so entirely given over to society as the girl of the broad chin and high-piled hair. . . .
>
> As I say, she is tall enough to look down on most men, does so, in fact, very often with head tilted back and her eyes half-closed—not at all the kind of girl you would choose to quarrel with. On the whole, I prefer her to the one of the broad chin. She is more serious, perhaps, and you must keep keyed pretty high to enjoy her society. But somehow you feel that she is a "man's woman" and would stand by a fellow and back him up if things should happen.[2]

Several of Norris' early stories are closely related to this idea of a "man's woman." They portray either the man who lacks such a woman and therefore decays ("A Caged Lion," August 20, 1894) or a woman who backs up a man and thereby intensifies his strength of will and purpose ("Thoroughbred," February, 1895). More often, however, his early stories are only indirectly related to the theme of a "man's woman," for they deal primarily with young men who accomplish heroic tasks when inspired by an attractive and good girl ("Travis Hallett's Half-Back," January, 1894).

The image of correct masculinity which emerges from these stories is that of the vigorous and the outdoors, of great deeds and of strength of body and mind. One of Norris' earliest articles in the *Wave*, written in the summer of 1895, clearly expresses this image. In reporting a day's amateur horse racing at Del

Monte, Norris contrasted the jockeys with the men at the ball later that evening, and cried out,

> Let us have men who are masculine, men who have other things to think of besides fooling away their time in ballrooms. After all, *think* of a man who smells of perfume and sachet—one's gorge rises at it! I would rather a man smell of horse sweat, the nasty salt rime, the bitter, pungent lather that gathers when the girths gall and the check strap chafes.[3]

This sharp distinction in Norris' mind between the world of perfume and that of horse sweat was sharpened even further during his *Wave* years by his reaction to the San Francisco literary scene of that time. Throughout the nineties, the English cult of aesthetic decadence, associated with Wilde, Beardsley, and the *Yellow Book,* was opposed by a cult of manliness, led by Kipling and W. E. Henley.[4] The first of these movements reached San Francisco in the form of Les Jeunes, a group of aesthetic young men who published between 1895 and 1897 a magazine called *The Lark,* which, though not decadent, was decidedly precious.[5] Although Norris was friendly with the two leading spirits of Les Jeunes, Gelett Burgess and Bruce Porter, he was displeased that *The Lark* should be taken as an expression of San Francisco literature. In his *Wave* essay "An Opening for Novelists" (May 22, 1897), he called for a masculine, Kiplingesque literature of San Francisco.

> Les Jeunes. Yes, there are Les Jeunes, and *The Lark* was delight-ful—delightful fooling, but there's a graver note and a more virile to be sounded. Les Jeunes can do better than *The Lark.* Give us stories now, give us men, strong, brutal men, with red-hot blood in 'em, with unleashed passions rampant in 'em, blood and bones and viscera in 'em, and women, too, that move and have their being. . . . It's the Life that we want, the vigorous, real thing, not the curious weaving of words and the polish of literary finish. . . . We don't want literature, we want life.[6]

Norris, in short, rejected aestheticism because it appeared to be antithetical to a literature centered on man's violent expression of his animal nature. Like Kipling in *The Light That Failed*, Norris associated the best in art with action and with firsthand experience rather than with education, society, or cities. And Norris himself tried to answer his own call for a San Francisco Kipling by writing in the months that followed this essay many stories which stressed the exceptional and violent. It is probable, therefore, that *Moran*, which is above all a story of "blood and bones and viscera," and which Norris began in late 1897, derives at least partly from Norris' impulse to write not only stories of "life not literature," but a novel as well.

Moran, however, is also a product of Norris' personal aspirations and difficulties in 1897, many of which he later recorded in *Blix*. This novel, as well as other sources, tells us that after he and Jeannette Black had known each other for over a year, they decided in the summer of 1897 that they were in love and that Norris would have to begin thinking more seriously about his literary career if they were to marry. Norris reacted to this decision in several ways. First, he sent off to an Eastern publisher a collection of his Kiplingesque *Wave* stories called "Ways That Are Dark."[7] Then, after Jeannette had left for school in October, he went off to Placer County to finish *McTeague*. Sometime in December, apparently, he learned that his collection was rejected, but, as the incident goes in *Blix*, the letter from the publisher went on to say that "the best selling book just now is the short novel—say thirty thousand words—of action and adventure. Judging from the stories of your collection, we suspect that your talent lies in this direction, and we would suggest that you write such a novel and submit the same to us" (III, 24).

Realizing that *McTeague* was not a novel he could depend on to launch a literary career, Norris turned to the writing of the kind of novel the publisher had suggested. The successful adventure novels which Norris knew and liked best were Kipling's *Captains Courageous* (1897), Davis' *Soldiers of Fortune* (1897), and Stevenson's *The Wrecker* (1892). But though these could serve as guides, Norris still needed an independent "yarn," as he called an adventure plot. At this point he probably recalled his visit to Captain Joseph Hodgson, a retired sea captain in charge of a lifesaving station in San Francisco Bay. During the summer of 1897, he and Jeannette had visited Hodgson for a *Wave* article on the lifesaving service, and the old captain had entertained them with many yarns, including one about how he "had captured a crew of Chinamen shark-fishing in Magdalena Bay, and had been nearly murdered by his men."[8] To this core of free booting adventure off the coast of Lower California, Norris added much from his favorite popular novels. The most important borrowing was from *Captains Courageous*, in which an effete young boy is washed overboard from a liner. He is picked up by a Grand Banks fishing boat and gradually acquires a masculine force of character from the hardships and responsibilities he experiences on the boat. From *The Wrecker* Norris borrowed the adventure story formula of swift narrative packed with mystery, disputed treasure, and bloodshed, while *Soldiers of Fortune* suggested to him a love triangle in which a girl with masculine inclinations (she drives locomotives in Davis' novel) wins the hero despite the rivalry of a more beautiful society girl. In short, Norris found in these novels plot material involving love, adventure, and initiation into masculinity which was readily adaptable both to his basic yarn and to his ideas about love and adventure. He therefore approached the novel with a certain gusto, though at the same time he recognized its inherent limitations.

Moran began appearing in the *Wave* on January 8, 1898.

Norris wrote each of its weekly installments no more than a few weeks before publication, and he also seems to have sent portions of the novel as it appeared to Doubleday and McClure, his "Eastern publisher." In mid-February, S. S. McClure responded by inviting Norris to come to New York to work on *McClure's Magazine* and the McClure newspaper syndicate. Norris eagerly accepted, though his move caused him to fall behind in the serial.[9] Meanwhile, the *Maine* had been sunk on February 16. In his chapters of March 26 and April 2 (chapters XI and XII) Norris wrote the event into the plot of *Moran* as a possible outlet for Moran and Wilbur's heroic endeavors after they had disposed of the Chinese bandit population of Lower California. But Norris had also been troubled about what to do with Moran—to kill her off or to allow her to go filibustering with Wilbur in Cuba.[10] He finally decided that she should die, and this decision, coupled with the fact that the Spanish-American War was over by the time the novel appeared in September, led him to cut most of the *Maine* allusions from chapters XI and XII. Otherwise, the published novel differs little from its *Wave* serialization.

As his titles suggest, Norris' focus in *Moran*, *Blix*, and *A Man's Woman* was on the chief female character in each of these novels, and, more particularly, on her role in aiding the central male character to achieve a correct masculinity. Within this process the woman also changes, though Norris above all emphasized her function in the transformation of the male.

In *Moran*, Ross Wilbur is initially an attender of teas and yachting parties, a man whose male force and gravity have been dulled by the feminine world of social convention and affectation. After being shanghaied, he is forced to rely on his strength and wits, until finally—with the fight against the Chinese pirates at Magdalena Bay—he has completely adapted to an eighth-century world of primitive barbarism, in which strength, brutality, and treachery are required to survive. Moran herself is the most striking symbol of this world and its values, and her function in the rationale of the novel is to inspire Wilbur by her actions and ideas to develop a masculine strength and courage. In short, the novel opens with Wilbur in a feminine role, Moran in a masculine one. (Clothes are important here. Wilbur is "reborn" when he sheds his gentlemanly dress for rough sailor clothing, and Moran is at first mistaken for a man because of her male clothing.) It is only when Wilbur conquers Moran by brute physical strength that he acquires a full masculinity in which he assumes from her the masculine qualities of leadership and of strength of purpose. Moran, on the other hand, not only surrenders her earlier masculinity when she is conquered, but also achieves femininity for the first time. She is "just a woman now" (III, 298), she tells Wilbur, and having lost her earlier strength and independence, she relies on him for protection and centers her attention on helping him fulfill his goals, whatever they are. Wilbur, with his newly gained seriousness, rejects the effete San Francisco world for the man's work of filibustering in Cuba.

The novel thus embodies a coherent masculine-feminine ethic. Man's correct role is that of a "man's man"—a man whose strength of mind and body aid him in "doing things," in performing a vigorous activity of any kind so long as the product of that activity is vaguely beneficial. Woman's correct function is that of a "man's woman"—to encourage man to affirm his masculinity by herself representing its qualities. But once the man achieves his full masculinity, the woman surrenders to his now superior strength. By her surrender, however, she not only gains love and sexuality (Norris carefully stresses the asexuality of Moran before Wilbur conquers her), but also a protector and a new role of "backing up" her mate in his endeavors and interests. With her surrender, the dynamic of the ethic is complete, since both parties now have static and permanent roles.

Norris' masculine-feminine ethic is inseparable from his primitivistic anti-intellectualism.[11] To Norris, masculinity signified action and force rather than thought or sophistication. His popular novels thus contain antithetical poles of value. His world of masculine strength is that of nature, emotion, instinct, and action; his world of feminine weakness consists of the city, thought, and indolence. Moran not only symbolizes the positive pole of this antithesis by her primitive appearance and behavior, but is a spokesman for it as well. She tells Wilbur, " 'I've lived by doing things, not by thinking things, or reading about what other people have done or thought; and I guess it's what you do that counts, rather than what you think or read about' " (III, 234).

Yet the novel embodies what may be called a half-way rather than a full primitivism. Many readers of *Moran* have been troubled by the ethics of Wilbur's growth in that he quadruples "all his strength, moral and physical" (III, 290), by stabbing a man to death and by mauling a woman. Norris sets these incidents, however, at Magdalena Bay, which he has established as an eighth-century world in which strength is the only law. In this primitive world, Wilbur discovers within himself the masculine strength of "the half-brute of the stone age" (III, 285), and that strength takes an appropriately savage form. But just as the journey to Magdalena Bay was a journey into man's past, so the return to San Francisco is a return to the present. In this world of the present, Wilbur can use his newly discovered masculinity, but Norris suggests that it will take forms appropriate to his own time, such as praiseworthy nationalistic efforts in the Caribbean. In a sense, Norris has allegorized the conventions of romance (struggle and bloodshed in an exotic setting), for he makes the killing of an enemy above all a symbol of man's brute past and of the strength developed in the past which is still available and necessary in the present. But Norris, like most allegorists, desires that it should be his theme, not its literal representation, which should be taken seriously.

Despite this possible defense of the ethics of *Moran,* Norris himself was troubled by the implications of the struggle at Magdalena Bay. He therefore hedged somewhat, first by making the Chinese pirates blatant symbols of evil, and then by having Wilbur slightly drunk all through the fight. Moreover, his decision to kill off Moran at the end of the novel suggests that his inability to find a role for her in the modern world was more than a failure in plot. He seems to have realized that the eighth century was not a fully acceptable source of value and behavior for the nineteenth—that Wilbur had absorbed what he could from her world, but that he could not really escape from the needs of his own, just as she was enclosed by the limitations of hers. Finally, in *A Man's Woman* Norris appears to be looking back ruefully at *Moran,* for in that later novel he created an eighth-century figure who has to learn a nineteenth-century humility and unselfishness.

As far as the art of *Moran* is concerned, the less said the better. It is a successful example of its genre, but its genre—because of its inherent limitations—compels little serious attention. Norris keeps up a steady pace of fresh adventures and crises, and he plots the novel with sufficient care so that the love story and the initiation theme reach a simultaneous climax in the battle at Magdalena Bay. But, given the superficiality of the characters and incidents of *Moran,* these successes make little difference in the total impact of the work. The novel, moreover, has a major technical flaw, one which Norris himself recognized.[12] Although Moran dominates the scene, the story is told through Wilbur, and he occupies our attention when we are really interested in Moran. She herself has a piquant fascination—what other heroine in American fiction coolly files down the teeth of her opponent to make him talk?—but she loses our interest when she becomes "just a woman." Despite the implicit seriousness of the theme of *Moran*, it is difficult to take the novel seriously, and one wonders whether Norris himself took it so, except perhaps as a way of getting East. One scene in particular sticks in the memory, a scene in which the long-lost Wilbur, bloody dirks slipping from his belt, is carried triumphantly into a full-dress ball by naval officers in gold and white uniforms, while a group of his former classmates give the Yale cheer. This is either a parody of the romantic adventure novel or one of the best examples of its absurdities.

2

Blix's sources are almost entirely autobiographical. The novel, which deals primarily with the romance between a young San Francisco writer and his girl, chronicles events that occurred in the summer and early fall of 1897, when Norris and Jeannette Black became engaged. It also includes much on Norris' career as a *Wave* reporter and on his writing of *Moran*.

It is not certain when Norris wrote *Blix*. He had little time for it between mid-March, 1898, when he finished *Moran*, and late April, when he became a war correspondent for McClure, though he may have begun it during that interval. In August he returned to San Francisco from Cuba to recuperate from a fever, and his release from reporting as well as his reunion with Jeannette probably stimulated him to work on the novel. Once back in New York in mid-October, he must have quickly finished it,[13] for it began appearing serially in March, 1899, and Norris spent most

Moran of the Lady Letty, Blix, AND *A Man's Woman*

of the winter of 1898-99 working on *A Man's Woman. Blix* appeared initially in *The Puritan,* a popular woman's magazine edited by Juliet Wilbor Tompkins, a former colleague of Norris' on the *Wave.* Its publication in this journal suggests that Norris was encouraged by Miss Tompkins to write a popular love story for her magazine, just as McClure, his "Eastern publisher," had encouraged him to write a popular adventure story.

Blix clarifies Norris' masculine-feminine ethic by normalizing the plot and characters in which it appears and by dealing more fully with the relationship between masculinity and moral force. In *Moran,* though Wilbur felt a "sudden quadrupling" of his moral strength after his transformation to masculinity, his moral growth is unconvincing and ambiguous. In *Blix,* however, Condy Rivers' weakness early in the novel is not only a lack of purpose and seriousness, but also an explicit moral laxity in his gambling, a vice which Norris frequently used to symbolize a general moral flabbiness. *Blix's* role is similar to Moran's. First, she leads Condy back to the "natural" world of sincerity and away from the conventional social world of parties and flirtations. Their unaffected relationship, and their fishing trips and their walks to the Presidio and explorations of San Francisco, are the thematic equivalents, within a courtship novel, of the blunt, open relationship between Moran and Wilbur during their adventures at Magdalena Bay. (Indeed, Norris introduces a mild Kiplingesque flavor of the strange and the exotic into their adventures and into the San Francisco setting.) Gradually, Blix inspires Condy, by her masculine force of character and purpose and by her interest in his improvement, to become strong enough both to fight his desire to gamble and to pursue his career with energy and perseverance. Blix is "the kind of girl that are the making of men," Condy tells her at one point (III, 105). As a result of her influence, the novel ends with "all the fine, virile, masculine energy of him . . . aroused

97

and rampant" (III, 171). He has conquered his vice and has seriously undertaken his life's work as a writer. At this point, as in *Moran*, the man's newly acquired masculinity is accompanied by the woman's discovery of her love and of her sexuality and by her transformation to a dependent femininity. Condy and Blix prepare to leave the "garden" of their courtship for marriage and the trials of life,

> And as they stood there, facing the gray and darkening Eastern sky, their backs forever turned to the sunset, Blix drew closer to him, putting her hand in his, looking a little timidly into his eyes. But his arm was around her, and the strong young force that looked into her eyes from his gave her courage (III, 174).

In both *Moran* and *Blix* man is reborn to masculinity with the aid of a "man's woman," who herself then achieves a true femininity. In *Blix*, however, Norris more clearly established the connection between a "man's woman" and moral development. Blix aids the moral growth of Condy in two ways. First, her purity and goodness help Condy to recognize his own moral potential. By knowing and responding to her goodness, he "felt his nobler side rousing up and the awakening of the desire to be his better self" (III, 129). But Blix emphasizes to Condy that the key to the development of his "nobler side" is strength. " 'What's a good man if he's weak?' " she asks him—" 'if his goodness is better than he is himself? It's the good man who is strong—as strong as his goodness and who can make his goodness count— who is the right kind of man' " (III, 56). Norris' ideal "man's woman" (and Blix represents that ideal more than does Moran) thus embodies both halves of a correct ethical balance—a feminine spiritual purity or moral awareness and a masculine strength —and she encourages man in the development of a similar balance in his own moral character.

As in *Moran,* Norris associates masculinity with primitivism, though in *Blix* nature rather than violence is the primary source and symbol of the primitive masculinity available to all men. Both Ross Wilbur and Condy Rivers discover their masculinity by rejecting the artificiality of "civilization," but whereas for Wilbur the climactic moment of discovery occurs during a life and death struggle, for Condy it occurs when he is in the presence of the turbulent Pacific shore. This moment is anticipated in *Blix* when Norris establishes nature as the matrix for that direct, emotional experience of life which is a necessary prelude for grasping the essential truths of life. As Condy and Blix walk along the shore,

> The simple things of the world, the great, broad primal emotions of the race stirred in them. As they swung along, going toward the ocean, their brains were almost as empty of thought or of reflection as those of two fine, clean animals. They were all for the immediate sensation; they did not think—they *felt* (III, 123).

At the close of the novel, when Condy and Blix have declared their love, they again view the Pacific.

> There was no detail in the scene. There was nothing but the great reach of the ocean floor, the unbroken plane of blue sky, and the bare green slope of land—three immensities, gigantic, vast, primordial. It was no place for trivial ideas and thoughts of little things. The mind harked back unconsciously to the broad, simpler, basic emotions, the fundamental instincts of the race (III, 168).

The assumptions of this scene are boldly primitivistic—that man discovers the essential truths of life when in immediate emotional contact with the immensities of nature, with nature acting as both an inspiration and a confirmation of these truths. In this setting, Condy and Blix discover the true meaning of their love, just as Annixter does in a similar setting in *The Octopus*. They realize that love is not an end but a beginning—that the responsibilities of marriage and of full manhood and womanhood await them. Here, then, in the context of a popular love story, Norris moves toward the theme of man's transcendental relationship with nature which figures so importantly in his trilogy of the wheat.

Norris' optimistic presentation of man's sensual nature in *Blix* makes the novel almost the antithesis of *Vandover*. Unlike Vandover, who falls into animal baseness, Condy—with the aid of a man's woman—discovers his animal strength and conquers his moral flaw. The autobiographical foundation of both novels, however, does not mean that Norris felt himself damned when he wrote *Vandover* and saved when he wrote *Blix*. Although his love for Jeannette was no doubt partly responsible for the changed stress in the two novels, the change is also inseparable from a large, coherent shift in Norris' interests within his theme of man's ethical dualism. Norris chose to dramatize various aspects of this theme at different times in his career within a broad movement from the destructive to the beneficial potentialities of man's dual nature. His own emotional state at the time he wrote a particular novel was only one strand in a complex web of motives prompting this choice. For example, Norris was suffused with Zola novels in 1894 when he wrote *Vandover*, while *Blix* is a consciously popular love story, and these facts are as significant as Norris' personal state of "salvation" in 1898. In any case, Norris himself seems to have recognized the antithetical relationship between the two novels. The key women in the two works have parallel roles and similar names. Vandover falls partly because he loses the influence of Turner Ravis, while Condy is saved by Travis Bessemer (Blix).

Norris' treatment of the relationship between Blix and Condy

raises the question of his portrayal of love. Does he reject sex as
a part of love and thereby exhibit—as several critics have charged
—a genteel, puritan attitude toward sex, seeing it as inherently
abhorrent and evil?[14] I believe that in *Blix* his depiction of love
is defensible on two grounds. First, Condy and Blix have decided,
as the novel opens, that their newfound code of sincerity pre-
cludes any casual flirtation or expression of love. They will be
chums, they decide, and their good-natured camaraderie throughout the novel, until they fall in love, is thus appropriate rather
than forced. Norris, moreover, indicates a sexual tension between
Condy and Blix, despite their predominantly asexual comrade-
ship. He does this, as was his habit, by emphasizing a particular
feminine characteristic of Blix and by having Condy's response
to that characteristic symbolize his sexual involvement. In *Mc-
Teague*, Trina's hair was such a characteristic; in *Blix*, it is Blix's
"barely perceptible delicious feminine odour" (III, 5). *Blix*, to be
sure, is not a profound study of love. But given its plot device
of lighthearted courtship and its faint suggestion of sexuality,
neither is it sufficient evidence that Norris regarded true love as
asexual. Norris, as we shall see in *The Octopus*, does not reject
sex. Rather, he makes the not unusual distinction between sexual
desire as a purely physical phenomenon and sexual desire as an
aspect of love leading to marriage. This distinction, of course, has
a middle-class, puritan cast, but it is far from being the extreme
Calvinistic guilt feeling about sex sometimes attributed to
Norris.[15]

Blix is a useful work for those concerned with Norris' biography, but this value does not make it a successful novel. Certainly, however, it succeeds more than either *Moran* or *A Man's
Woman*, for it lacks the improbability of the first and the tedious
prolixity of the second. The reader's enjoyment of it depends
primarily on his response to its theme of courtship as a time of

high spirits, of delight in raillery, of pleasure in each other's company at moments of repose and of excitement. It is courtship idealized, with the ideal incorporating a steady movement toward self-discovery, love, and marriage, and with all problems solved by good fortune, hard work, and love. Its tone is that of an idyllic moment in life, and the pleasure of reading it is like the pleasure of hearing a lighthearted boating song. Perhaps most of all it is courtship as one might imagine it, though it is seldom so, and thus its primary appeal is as fantasy. Indeed, if one thinks of the novel in this way, one can respond openly to its charm, and, as with most fantasy, one can neglect its limited view of experience. But like most fantasy, it is soon forgotten.

3

A *Man's Woman*, a novel about the romance between a strong-willed Arctic explorer and an equally strong-willed nurse, has a complex history. Two of Norris' earliest stories, "Unequally Yoked" (September 22, 1893) and "A Caged Lion" (August 20, 1894), deal with an explorer whose vocation is destroyed by a trivial-minded, possessive wife. In another story, one of a series called "Man Proposes" (July 4, 1894), Norris told of a man and a woman on a sinking yacht. Believing that they are doomed, the man asks for an avowal of her love, and she, thinking that a lie in this instance could do no harm and might bring him a little final happiness, tells him that she loves him. A few minutes later, they are saved. Norris ends the story at this point, leaving the reader to speculate on the outcome of this harmless and benevolent lie. A *Man's Woman* stems from these three stories; it deals with a woman's relationship to masculine heroism, and its central plot complication arises out of a similar, though somewhat different, benevolent lie.

Norris' "The End of the Beginning" (September 4, 1897) contains a third major element in *A Man's Woman*—its Arctic material. In this story, the plot of the benevolent lie is shifted to an Arctic expedition. Norris could not help being aware of Arctic exploration, which was as much a matter of public interest in the late nineteenth century as space exploration is today, and which involved much the same combination of national rivalry and personal heroism. But Norris' immediate stimulus to use his benevolent lie plot in a new setting was his meeting with Captain Hodgson, the old sailor who had told him about fighting pirates in Lower California and who himself appears as a character in *Blix.* Hodgson had been a member of the expedition sent in search of Lieutenant-Commander George W. De Long and the *Jeannette.* De Long had attempted to reach the Pole by the unorthodox route of the Bering Strait and Siberia, but had been frozen in for two years. At last, in 1882, his ship was crushed, and he had marched over the ice in a desperate attempt to reach the coast of Siberia. He himself finally perished, though some of the crew, including George Melville, the chief engineer, were saved. Norris was sufficiently interested in Hodgson's account of the *Jeannette* disaster to look up several books on it and to use this material in his story.[16] Melville's *In the Lena Delta* (1885) and Mrs. De Long's edition of her husband's ice journals, *The Voyage of the Jeannette* (1887), supplied Norris with the narrative of the retreat over the ice used in both "The End of the Beginning" and *A Man's Woman.* But Norris also wanted to include an Arctic rescue in his story, and the rescue of the *Jeannette* survivors was not the spectacular, last-minute affair he needed for his benevolent lie plot. He turned, therefore, to W. S. Schley's *The Rescue of Greely* (1885) and Adolphus Greely's *Three Years of Arctic Service* (1886), both of which contain vivid accounts of the rescue in 1884 of the half-dead survivors of Greely's expedition. These four books gave Norris both the exciting adventures and the rich detail which help to make the Arctic chapters of *A Man's Woman* effective and memorable. There is no evidence, however, that Ward Bennett, Norris' Arctic explorer, is modeled on either De Long or Greely, or, indeed, on such other Arctic explorers as Nansen or Peary.

Norris may have had some vague idea in 1897, when he wrote "The End of the Beginning," that he might expand the story into a novel, but he did not begin thinking seriously about such a project until the summer of 1898, when he returned to San Francisco from Cuba. Jeannette Black had been interested in a possible career as a nurse or doctor (this gets into *Blix* as well), and Norris himself had written an article on nursing for the *Wave* in 1896.[17] It was Jeannette, then—or so it seems from Norris' inscription to her in a copy of the novel[18]—who in the summer of 1898 suggested to Norris the possibility of a novel combining Arctic exploration and nursing—a novel in which the benevolent lie situation of "The End of the Beginning" would introduce a love story between a nurse and an Arctic explorer. *A Man's Woman*, thus, is as full of sickroom "business" as it is of dogsledding and pemmican. For his detailed information about hip bone excisions and typhoid fever, Norris went to his old fraternity brother, Albert J. Houston, who had just graduated from medical school.

It was probably also with some encouragement from S. S. McClure that Norris undertook the novel after his return to New York and after he had completed *Blix*. Arctic exploration was popular material in the nineties, and *McClure's Magazine* carried many articles and stories on it during this period. Five Polar expeditions were launched in 1898, including one by Peary, and the Spanish-American War had so much inflated national pride that to many Americans having an American reach the

Pole was more important than reaching it at all—a fervor which Norris himself shares in the closing chapters of the novel. But despite this encouragement, and despite his own initial enthusiasm, the writing of the novel proceeded slowly. After its first two chapters of Arctic adventure, the work settled down to what Norris later called "niggling analysis" of his two central characters.[10] Nevertheless, he finished the novel in March, 1899, and it was syndicated by McClure during that year, first in the *San Francisco Chronicle* and then in the *New York Sun*. In these versions Norris included a very detailed description of a hip operation—much sawing of bones and cutting of arteries—which offended some readers. When the novel appeared in book form in February, 1900, this description was replaced by a less bloody one, but otherwise the book version differs little from the newspaper publication.

If *Moran* introduces Norris' masculine-feminine ethic, and *Blix* amplifies it, *A Man's Woman* corrects any possible misunderstanding of it. At the opening of this novel, Ward Bennett and Lloyd Searight appear to have already achieved their proper roles—indeed, she is called a "man's woman," he a "man's man" (VI, 16, 34). A courageous and iron-willed Arctic explorer, he is strikingly masculine, while she, having disdained affectation and petty interests, is aiding the world's work as a nurse. Norris desired in this novel, however, not only to glorify these roles, but also to point out their inherent dangers. Most of all, he demonstrated that a Bennett can become the victim of his iron resolve, that a fixed resolution can embody a bestial selfishness and blindness as well as a praiseworthy purposefulness. Bennett's career in the Arctic had conditioned him to respond to all opposition as forces to be subdued, since the ice, cold, and distances of the Arctic are insensate obstacles which must be overcome if he is to survive. Norris symbolizes them as the Enemy, and they call forth the singlemindedness of men in battle. Lloyd has also fought against an unreasoning Enemy—disease rather than ice—and has also developed a firm will. Her error is to mistake strength for independence, to center herself too exclusively on her own career and her own work. Like Bennett, she has allowed strength to narrow into pride and selfishness.

In the central scene of the novel, these two powerful and fiercely independent wills clash when Bennett insists that Lloyd leave a patient dangerously ill with an infectious disease. As in *Moran*, the man conquers, though now by strength of purpose rather than physical power. Lloyd for the first time begins to realize the "intended natural weakness of the woman" (VI, 120). As she surrenders, her love emerges clearly. But with her love and capitulation, Bennett must assume responsibility for her well-being. It is on this basis that Lloyd appeals to Bennett to reconsider his demand that she leave—that his obligations include her spiritual as well as her physical welfare, and that to leave would violate her "code of life." She tells him:

> "I am all different now. I am not the woman I was a half hour ago. You must be brave for me now, and you must be strong for me and help me to do my duty. We must live up to the best that is in us and do what we think is right, no matter what risks we run, no matter what the consequences are. I would not have asked you to help me before—before what has happened—but now I need your help" (VI, 129).

Bennett, however, rejects the full responsibility of his new role and almost destroys Lloyd's love for him by forcing her to do something which she knows is wrong.

With this scene, Lloyd has discovered her correct feminine role of submission, though her pride is not fully chastened until she goes through a humiliating confession to her fellow nurses that she has left a patient. Bennett, meanwhile, gradually realizes that he may have been mistaken in his demand, and that his monomaniacal intensity has not only conquered Lloyd but has also broken and violated her spirit by forcing her to be false to her sense of duty. For the first time in his life he faces the possibility that force may not be enough, that human beings are not objects to be subjected blindly to his will. As with Lloyd, his pride and his supreme self-confidence are shaken, and like her he makes humiliating confessions of his error to others. In short, the bulk of the novel is devoted to the process by which a strong-willed woman learns to win love by surrendering and a strong-willed man learns to temper strength with understanding. Or, put in another way, the novel affirms that selfishness and pride—characteristics often disguised as firmness of will—must be overcome if love is to flourish. "Was not the struggle with one's self the greatest fight of all," Lloyd concludes after her confession to her fellow nurses, "greater, far greater, than had been the conflict between Bennett's will and her own?" (VI, 182).

In both characters, then, Norris amends some of the implications of his earlier dramatizations of masculinity and femininity. He now stresses that masculinity is not simply brute force and that femininity is not a New-Woman indifference to domesticity or a preoccupation with one's own career rather than the husband's. (Significantly, Lloyd gives up her profession when she marries Bennett.) It is only when Lloyd and Bennett have shed the excesses of their strength that the novel takes on the pattern of *Moran* and *Blix*. The last quarter of *A Man's Woman* contains the familiar business of Lloyd encouraging Bennett, now weakened by illness and by the blow to his self-assurance, to reassert his masculinity, to return to his career as an explorer. The novel closes as do *Moran* and *Blix*—the man about to begin a man's work, the woman, having achieved love and sexuality, fully occupied in the career of the man.

As in his other popular novels, Norris in A *Man's Woman* carefully established the primitivistic sources of the strength and insight of his major characters. Bennett in the Arctic, like Ross Wilbur at Magdalena Bay, is an eighth-century man, "a giant, an ogre, a colossal jotun hurling ice blocks, fighting out a battle unspeakable, in the dawn of the world, in chaos and in darkness" (VI, 24). But unlike *Moran*, which uncritically celebrates this primitive ferocity, A *Man's Woman* goes on to develop its limitations in the modern world. Back in civilization, Bennett kills a runaway horse with a blow from his geologist's hammer, and Norris comments:

> There was a primitiveness, a certain hideous simplicity in the way Bennett had met the situation. . . . The vast, brutal direct-ness of the deed was out of place and incongruous at this end-of-the-century time. It ignored two thousand years of civilization. It was a harsh, clanging, brazen note, powerful, uncomplicated, which came jangling in, discordant and inharmonious with the tune of the age. It savoured of the days when men fought the brutes with their hands or with their clubs (VI, 91).

Norris here limits the range and nature of the dog-eat-dog brutality of Ross Wilbur, and indeed of Charlie Geary in *Vandover* as well, by imposing the test of civilization on man's primitivism. Men still require strength of will, but, as Norris makes clear in A *Man's Woman*, civilization has reached a point at which strength must be controlled by understanding, unselfishness, and reason. The moral and physical conditions of the Arctic are not those of a late-nineteenth-century American city.

Lloyd's central values are also primitive and anti-intellectual. Like Moran and Blix, her creed is "to do things, not to think them; to do things, not to talk them; to do things, not to read them. No matter how lofty the thoughts, how brilliant the talk, how beautiful the literature—for her, first, last, and always, were acts, acts, acts—concrete, substantial, material acts" (VI, 49). Acts, but also emotions—for like Condy and Blix, she has a moment of transcendental insight into her own nature and into the great truths of life. She sits before an open window and looks out into an orchard. "By degrees the thinking faculties of her brain, as it were, a myriad of delicate interlacing wheels, slowly decreased in the rapidity and intensity of their functions. She began to feel instead of to think" (VI, 192). In this state she rediscovers her love for Bennett and also the beauty and sweetness of love.

In *A Man's Woman* Norris has thus come a considerable distance from *Moran* in his treatment of man's nonintellectual faculties. Now he imposes serious controls on man's animal force. He still calls for a life of action, but he now also places great stress on what might be called a transcendental epistemology— that is, that great personal and universal truths are derived emotionally, with the intellect in suspension. This is still primitive anti-intellectualism, to be sure, in which emotion and action take precedence over thought. But at this point Norris has shifted his interest from man's "lower" to his "higher" nonintellectual qualities. He is not so much now concerned with the brute ferocity of the struggle for existence as with the possibilty that man as a higher being can live a higher life. He has shifted, in other words, from Geary's instinctive drive for power to Lloyd's sublimation of self and to her transcendental faculty. His full expression of this shift comes only in his treatment of Presley, Annixter, and Vanamee in *The Octopus,* but it is firmly anticipated in his popular novels.

A Man's Woman, despite its value to a historian of Norris' ideas, is his worst novel. Its failure is due to Norris' inability to bring alive the abstract thesis on which the novel rests. A key to this inability lies in his handling of setting. Unlike his other novels, all of which have a definite locale, A Man's Woman is set in an imaginary city which is described as an abstraction (The City). Its setting lacks the sharpness and flavor of Norris' rendering of San Francisco or even Chicago. Similarly, Norris was unable to give fictional reality to the characters and incidents within his abstract plot line of two wills colliding, parting, and then joining. He could infuse theme into a concrete situation, as he did with the Collins murder in McTeague or with the Mussel Slough massacre in The Octopus. But once he disposed of his Arctic material in A Man's Woman, he had to create situations to embody a thesis, and his characters became puppets and his action became contrived and implausible.

The key scene in the novel, in which Bennett forces Lloyd to leave her patient, illustrates the weakness of the work as a whole. The scene is laboriously prepared for by forced coincidences and elaborate plotting in order to reach the improbable situation of Lloyd nursing Bennett's best friend, Ferriss, although Bennett is unaware of the patient's identity. When Bennett discovers that the patient is Ferriss, he must choose, in the best tradition of popular melodrama, between love and friendship. Slowly and painfully the scene reaches its climax. Meanwhile, as Lloyd and Bennett struggle for supremacy, Ferriss is lying unattended, and the reader at last loses patience with everyone concerned, including Norris, and wishes that those two strong-willed characters would go to the devil so long as someone would look after the dying man. In short, by excessive melodrama, artifice, and abstraction, Norris loses our interest in his major characters and their dilemma—and thus in the entire novel.

4

Moran, Blix, and A Man's Woman explore what I have called a masculine-feminine ethic, in which men achieve a correct masculinity with the aid of women who themselves move from masculinity to femininity. Norris' heroines have masculine names and are tall and full-bodied not simply because Norris was fascinated by Viking types. Rather, their masculine names and physiques symbolize their masculine force—that they are women who want to "do things" rather than devote themselves to trivialities, and, most of all, that they have a strength and seriousness of character which it is their function to encourage in men. The fact that all three heroines affirm a life of action rather than of thought indicates, as I have noted, that Norris associated masculinity with the primitive, the felt, the "natural" rather than with either civilization or intellect—in other words, with an atavistic physical force which men first developed in fighting nature or their enemies but which they must continue to draw upon if they are to progress materially and morally. *A Man's Woman*, however, imposes limitations on sheer atavistic force, and thereby modifies and completes the ethic.

In all three novels, woman is the prime mover in man's transformation—without a "man's woman," Wilbur would be a San Francisco playboy, Condy Rivers a vice-ridden hack, and Bennett (after his illness) a "professor" rather than a "doer." Within this theme, Norris shifted his emphasis from woman's role in encouraging strength to her part in directing the uses of strength. In *Moran* he celebrated the emergence of the "half-brute" in Wilbur in order to dramatize sensationally the theme of masculinity. In *Blix* and *A Man's Woman*, he stressed that man is not simply a creature of conquest and of strong-willed gratification—that strength plays a major role in resisting temptation and that it must not be used cruelly or selfishly. Lloyd has a "larger, better nature" than Bennett, even after his self-abnegation, and, as with Blix, her function is "not only to call back his strength, but to guide it and direct [it] into its appointed channels" (VI, 209-210).

The three novels are weak not only because of their conventional and superficial plots of adventure and romantic fulfillment, but because of the inherent inadequacy of Norris' masculine-feminine ethic as a representation of the complex world of sexual relations. His themes of man as primitive conqueror and woman as reservoir of moral strength are heavily colored by popular nineteenth-century social and moral beliefs, particularly those which allotted unequal portions of the animal and spirit to man and woman. There is much in Norris of the nineteenth-century tendency to substitute woman for Christ as the hope and salvation of fallen man. Whatever the source of these themes, however, Norris dramatizes them shallowly and programmatically. His masculine-feminine ethic is moral in the narrow sense of the word: it tells us not so much about human beings as about conventions of social expectation, about the way men and women are supposed to act. Although such conventions interest the social historian, they limit the viability of the novel dominated by them. The novels occasionally rise above their weaknesses when Norris creates compelling sensational symbols of various aspects of his ethic (Moran, the Arctic) or when he neglects it entirely for the intrinsic appeal of scene and event (a good deal of *Blix* is successful on this level). The novels fail most obviously when Norris attempts to give the ethic a depth of analysis and dramatization it cannot bear.

Chapter Four

The Octopus AND The Pit

1

Norris conceived his trilogy of the wheat early in 1899, about the time he was finishing *A Man's Woman*. It occupied him until his death in October, 1902. As far as is known, the idea of a trilogy dealing with wheat sprang whole into Norris' mind. His first recorded mention of it, in a letter to Howells in March, 1899, contains the full conception:

> I think there is a chance for somebody to do some great work with the West and California as a background, and which will be at the same time thoroughly American. My Idea is to write three novels around the one subject of Wheat. First, a study of California (the producer), second, a study of Chicago (the distributor) third, a study of Europe (the consumer) and in each to keep to the idea of this huge, Niagara of wheat rolling from West to East. I think a big Epic trilogy *could* be made out of such a subject, that at the same time would be modern and distinctly American.[1]

Norris was writing to Howells to thank him for his review of *McTeague*, in which Howells had praised the novel for its honesty and strength but had criticized its unbalanced portrait of life. "Life is squalid and cruel and vile and hateful," Howells had written, "but it is also noble and tender and pure and lovely, too."[2] "You were quite right," Norris had admitted earlier in his letter, "in saying that the novel that is true to life cannot afford to ignore the finer things." Of course, Norris had included much that was "noble and tender" in his three popular novels, but he himself felt that these works were weak and inadequate. In November, 1899, when he was about to begin writing *The Octopus*, he wrote to I. F. Marcosson:

I am going back *definitely* now to the style of MacT. and stay with it right along. I've been sort of feeling my way ever since the "Moran" days and getting a twist of myself. Now I think I know where I am at and what game I play the best. The Wheat series will be straight naturalism with all the guts I can get into it.[3]

Two of Norris' primary motives, then, in his wheat trilogy were to return to the strength and depth of *Vandover* and *McTeague*—this is what he means by "straight naturalism" rather than any philosophical idea (note the "style" of *McTeague*[4])— and to present a more balanced view of man's failings and glories than had characterized his initial work. To achieve this more balanced view, Norris had only to draw upon some of the more optimistic qualities of Le Conte's evolutionary theism, those which he had already begun to develop in his popular novels. He could stress man's spiritual uniqueness rather than his animal past, and he could dramatize natural laws with greater emphasis on racial and social benefits than on individual destruction. These more affirmative ideas within Le Conte's thought were not entirely absent from Norris' earliest novels. Vandover, for example, has a spiritual as well as a sensual nature, and the natural law which destroys him benefits the race. The emphasis in the novel, however, is on Vandover's flawed will and on his destruction.

Norris' greater stress in his trilogy on the optimistic themes in evolutionary theism stemmed primarily from his own maturing exploration of his basic response to experience, though it was also probably influenced by the generally hostile reception of *Mc-Teague*.[5] His repeated demand that the novelist be sincere and responsible is not undermined, however, by his expression of a more "positive" world view in his trilogy. This view does not represent an abrupt shift in his thought, but—as I have suggested in several places—is rather the product of his constantly expanding dramatization of the basic ethical position present in his earliest work.

But the fact that this expansion was anticipated from the first does not mean that there were not forces and influences, such as the critical reception of his books or his engagement to Jeannette, which affected the nature and speed of its development. Another such force was Norris' friendship with the Reverend William Rainsford. Norris had met Rainsford early in 1898, soon after arriving in New York, and the two remained friends until Norris' death.[6] Rainsford, who was rector of St. George's church in lower Manhattan, had been influenced by Spencer, Drummond, and Fiske, and was an articulate and active evolutionary theist. He was also a muscular Christian who, like Charles Kingsley, believed in the social responsibility of the church and in the individual's responsibility to maintain a strong, active body.[7] (He himself was a big-game hunter.) Norris thought sufficiently well of Rainsford's ideas to recommend the publication of his sermons to Doubleday and to aid him in his social work.[8] Rainsford's strongly positive evolutionary view of man's relationship to nature and to God contained little that Norris had not found in Le Conte, but Rainsford's vibrant personality probably helped revivify this aspect of Le Conte's thought in Norris' mind.

Norris seems to have borrowed from Zola the idea that a series of thematically linked novels was the best means of encompassing a vast social or philosophical theme. Zola had written a series of twenty novels dealing with such a theme—the relationship between hereditary and social degeneration in the Second Empire. He had completed his Rougon-Macquart series in 1893, and had gone on to write two shorter sequences of linked novels—first *Les Trois Villes*, a trilogy of 1894-1898, and then *Les Quatre Evangiles*, an incomplete tetralogy of 1899-1902. Zola's practice was to have each novel in a series exist as an independent entity but to use reappearing characters. Norris rejected even this linking device, probably because of the difficulty in plotting such links between novels set in California, Chicago, and Europe, and because the absence of linking characters would emphasize the wheat as the dominant linking element.

Norris' choice of wheat as the subject of his trilogy was influenced jointly by Le Conte and Zola. Zola's object in much of his later work, particularly *La Terre*, had been to dramatize elaborate parallels between man and nature. He wished to affirm the unity of all life in order to celebrate the natural and to denigrate the artificial and the mechanical. Le Conte, too, had stated the unity of all life, and though he believed that this unity was achieved by God's universal presence, he nevertheless stressed that man could best know God by studying natural laws and processes. The combined impact of Zola and Le Conte, therefore, was to reemphasize the idea that Truth (that is, universal laws of life) could best be found in nature. Norris, however, was critical of Zola's abstract and polemical method in such later novels as *Fécondité*.[9] He was drawn more to the fictional method of *La Terre*, in which Zola used a vivid, sensational narrative and a dominant, massive symbol to make concrete and dramatic his epic theme of nature's eternal fecundity. Indeed, this novel, in which a wheat-raising area is the setting for the theme of the permanent richness of the land despite the pettiness of those fighting for its possession, was probably the initial stimulus for Norris' trilogy. Norris' attempt in his trilogy was to strive for the depth and sweep of Zola's later novels, but to do so within very particularized settings, narratives, and symbols. Much that is best in his epic of the wheat derives from his success in using wheat as a concrete symbol of man's relationship to nature and from his ability to translate such exciting events as the Mussel Slough tragedy and the Leiter wheat corner into fictional reality.

A good deal of the circumstantiality of *The Octopus* also stems from Norris' desire to write a new kind of regional novel. In his letter to Howells, he had noted that the first novel in his trilogy would use California and the West as a background and yet be "thoroughly American." In *The Octopus*, then, Norris strove for a regionalism in depth—for fiction which was regionally particularized but which had a national relevance as well. Many of the ideas about fiction which Norris expressed in his critical articles of 1901-1902 derive more from his writing of *The Octopus* than from theories which served as conscious guides during his planning and writing of that novel. But his later rejection of the Great American Novel and his call for a more penetrating regionalism than local color were articulated, guiding ideas for *The Octopus*.

There were, then, a variety of motives and influences bearing on Norris' initial concept of his trilogy, and an even greater variety, as will be seen, affecting each of the two novels he completed. But his overall plan was clear in his mind from the first: a trilogy of novels dealing with a concrete and seemingly limited and commonplace subject—the raising, marketing, and consuming of wheat—which, when explored in depth, would reveal great moral, racial, and national truths. Here was an opportunity for Norris to combine his genius for the particular with his capacity and need to reach out for the universal, and he responded to the opportunity with seriousness and intensity.

2

"A Story of California (the producer)," Norris had written Howells. During the 1870's and eighties, wheat had been the principal crop of the San Joaquin Valley, the long central plain of California. Norris was city born and bred, and though he had visited the San Joaquin while a *Wave* reporter,[10] he knew little about wheat farming. He also had only a sketchy knowledge of what he quickly decided would be the central incident of his novel, the armed battle in May, 1880, between agents of the Southern Pacific Railroad and wheat farmers of Tulare County in the southern San Joaquin. Clearly firsthand research was required, and Norris soon reached an agreement with Doubleday and McClure that he would receive full pay while he spent several months in California working up the background for the novel.

The Mussel Slough massacre, as it was called, stemmed from the practice of awarding railroad companies large tracts of public land adjoining their lines as a stimulus to railroad construction.[11] When the Southern Pacific built a line through the San Joaquin, it invited development of its land and promised to sell it to settlers at a nominal cost when the land was graded. Some years later, however, when the company priced its land, it did so—in a classic example of what Henry George called unearned increment—on the basis of its improved rather than its original value. The ranchers protested, and fought the Southern Pacific in the courts. They also organized an association to resist the railroad by force if need be. The Mussel Slough massacre resulted from the attempted dispossession of several ranchers from their land. A group of them halted the U. S. marshal and his party, and a fight broke out in which five ranchers and two men accompanying the marshal were killed. Although this incident occurred in 1880, its memory was kept alive throughout the 1880's and nineties by the railroad's dominant role in the state's economic and political life. When one recalls that throughout the late nineteenth century California merchants and farmers alike were completely dependent on the Southern Pacific's transportation monopoly for the movement of their products, that the company owned vast areas of land, and that its wealth and patronage gave it a decisive voice in state politics, it is not surprising that it was universally feared and hated and that the Mussel Slough affair was maintained in the public's imagination as a dramatic and sensational symbol of the railroad's destructive power.

It should be clear, however, that it was no sudden outburst of social consciousness which led Norris to an interest in the railroad trust. He had not evidenced any concern with contemporary social problems in his earlier novels, but he did not suddenly discover in 1899 that trusts, in Mr. Dooley's words, were "heejous monsters." It would have been impossible for him to live in California and escape some response to the role and power of the Southern Pacific. Norris' history teacher at the University of California, who was also a Congregational minister, had in 1894 dispassionately noted the "unaminous hatred of the people of California toward the Southern Pacific Company."[12] And Norris himself in *Vandover* had written that when Vandover returned from Harvard, times were hard and "one spoke bitterly of a certain great monopoly that was ruining both the city and the state."[13] Moreover, Norris' two years on the *Wave* had made the railroad's ubiquitousness in California a constant reality. The magazine had been founded by the Southern Pacific and still received a subsidy from it.

Norris' awareness and experience of social evil had no doubt broadened and deepened over the years. He had worked on *Mc-*

119

Clure's with such stalwart muckrakers as Ida Tarbell and Ray Stannard Baker,[14] and he had seen starvation and poverty in their grossest forms in Cuba.[15] But the appeal of the Mussel Slough massacre as the pivotal event in his novel was less the opportunity it offered for the depiction of social injustice than its literary usefulness. He wanted to write a novel about wheat, but a novel which would also have "the West and California as a background" and be "at the same time thoroughly American."[16] The Mussel Slough incident was therefore Norris' almost inevitable choice, for it combined in one sensational event the nucleus of a story about California wheat growers and the Southern Pacific with a chance to explore the larger problem of industrial monopoly in America.

Nor does Norris' interest in the Southern Pacific represent the kind of social consciousness which since the 1930's has been associated with the committed writer. By portraying the injustices of monopoly, Norris was scarcely dealing with a new or inflammatory or even distressing subject. Trusts had few defenders in late-nineteenth-century America except for a handful of economic theorists and the trust owners themselves, and the Southern Pacific had even fewer than most. Attacking a trust at that time represented little more social involvement than attacking Communism today.[17] Moreover, the victims of oppression in *The Octopus* are not comparable to the mill workers or fruit pickers in the proletarian novel of the 1930's. Norris included a few tenant farmers and railroad workers among these victims, but for the most part they are capitalists who have large investments in land and equipment and who are competing with the railroad for the riches of the land. Norris dramatized feelingly the plight of Minna Hooven, the daughter of a tenant farmer, who is driven into the streets by the trust's actions. But his sentiment here is primarily sympathy for the individual rather than for the class to which she belongs and for the condition of that class. Norris could always respond to individual hardship or pain, but he had little understanding of the day-to-day drudgery and bleakness of most working men. In 1902 he reported a strike in the Pennsylvania coal mines. He was only mildly sympathetic toward the miners, and thought that they were really well off, since they had good pay, cheap fuel, and short hours.[18] *The Octopus* is not a novel about the class war or about the downtrodden, though the struggle for wealth and the realities of economic power are part of its subject matter. It is more a novel about man's relationship to nature than a story of man as a social being, just as *McTeague* is a novel about man's animal past rather than about lower-class life.

Norris worked in California on the background of *The Octopus* from May to July, 1899. He then returned to New York and spent almost a year and a half preparing and writing the novel, completing it in December, 1900. He devoted more time and effort to *The Octopus* than to any of his other works. He looked up old accounts of the farmers' grievances and of the Mussel Slough affair in libraries and newspaper offices. He interviewed friends, railroad officials, and politicians, and he wrote numerous letters asking for specific information. He compiled several notebooks of newspaper clippings bearing on economic and social issues taken up in the novel.[19] As the novel progressed, he drew upon the work of other authors, upon scenes he had visited, and upon the characteristics of people he knew—in other words, upon the full range of his experience—for the particulars of the novel. A book could be written about the sources of *The Octopus*. I can do no more here than to offer first an example of how Norris used his sources and then a general sketch of the primary influences on the novel.

Toward the end of *The Octopus*, Norris juxtaposed the wanderings of Mrs. Hooven and the Gerard dinner party. As Mrs.

Hooven, the widow of a tenant farmer killed at Mussel Slough, begs with her child on the streets of San Francisco, Gerard, a vice-president of the P. & S. W. Railroad, gives an elaborate dinner party. The meal ends at the moment Mrs. Hooven is discovered dead of starvation. Norris was probably influenced by a similar incident in Zola's *Germinal,* in which a group of hungry miners are depicted in relation to a rich meal being served at the mine manager's house. But for much of the detail of his parallel narration of Mrs. Hooven and the dinner party, Norris drew upon two newspaper stories which he had clipped and then saved in his notebook. One was a story of a lavish dinner given by a Southern Pacific executive, the other of a mother starving to death on the streets of New York with her little daughter beside her.[20] In addition, Norris used a specific locale for both the dinner and Mrs. Hooven's wanderings. All of the Big Four—the founders of the Southern Pacific—had mansions on Nob Hill. Norris' detailed description of Gerard's house suggests that he used one of these mansions as his model—probably that of Mark Hopkins. Hopkins had built his house in the seventies, but in 1893 it had become the property of the San Francisco Art Association, which used it as a school and gallery.[21] Norris had visited it many times as a *Wave* reporter, and probably revisited it in 1899. Moreover, he carefully described Mrs. Hooven's journeying on the day of her death, so that it is clear that she dies on Nob Hill, probably only a few steps from the Gerard house.[22] He thus brought his bitterly ironic juxtaposition to an equally bitter geographically ironic close. Norris in this section of *The Octopus* used literary works, contemporary events, and personal knowledge of locale and scene. With some variation he used the same combination throughout the novel, whether he was portraying settings, characters, or events.

To go on to a more general account of the sources of *The*

Octopus, one of Norris' chief tasks in California was to look up newspaper reports of the massacre. These reports, which included full reviews of the farmers' grievances and the railroad's position, supplied him with much of the detail he later used in describing the dispute and its climax. The *Visalia Weekly Delta*, in particular, published column after column of eyewitness accounts of the Mussel Slough battle. These accounts were republished in the San Francisco papers, which Norris consulted at the Mechanics' Library and the offices of the *San Francisco Chronicle*.[23] Norris also wanted to observe the operation of a wheat ranch. His friend Ernest Peixotto arranged for him to visit the Santa Anita Ranch at Tres Pinos in San Bonito County. Tres Pinos was not in the San Joaquin, but in the rolling country northwest of the central valley. Since 1880, however, much of the San Joaquin had been converted to orchards and to other crops, which probably made it difficult for Norris to find a suitable ranch near Hanford, Visalia, or Tulare, the principal towns of the Mussel Slough area. But there is little doubt that he visited the southern San Joaquin, both for general impressions of the district and for a particular study of Tulare, which is one of the models for Bonneville, the bustling business town of *The Octopus*. The other model was Hollister, a town not far from the Santa Anita Ranch. Tres Pinos, moreover, was only a short distance from San Juan Bautista, one of the Camino Real mission towns. In *The Octopus* Norris depicted this decayed Spanish town, with its mission overlooking a seed ranch, as Guadalajara. For Tulare and Tipton, then, the two towns on the Southern Pacific line, Norris substituted Tulare and San Juan Bautista. He was thus able to suggest some of California's romantic past as well as to dramatize its present crisis.

Two of the principal scenes in *The Octopus* are the barn dance and the rabbit drive. Norris observed the first at Santa Anita, but there is some doubt whether he actually experienced the second, despite the vividness of his account. His friend Peixotto had in 1892 illustrated an article describing such a drive in the San Joaquin,[24] and Norris seems to have relied on this article for much of his detail. In general, however, he gained most of his wheat farming material from his stay with Mr. and Mrs. Ashe, the owners of the Santa Anita Ranch. Mrs. Ashe, who was from an old Spanish family, told Norris some of the legends of the area which he used in the novel and also served as a model for Mrs. Derrick. Norris did make use of one of his few earlier encounters with wheat, an account he had written for the *Wave* on the sailing of an Indian famine relief ship sponsored by a San Francisco committee.[25] He shaped this incident into the climax of the wheat harvest he had been observing at the Santa Anita Ranch.

In New York Norris continued to work steadily on another important background area of the novel—the political and economic details of the struggle between the ranchers and the railroad. He particularly needed information on the ranchers' grievances over freight rates and on their attempt to relieve their plight by legal and political action.[26] While in San Francisco he had interviewed Harry Wright, an old fraternity brother, for legal details, and a former *Wave* editorial writer, John P. Irish, for the railroad's position.[27] He had also started a notebook in which he kept articles dealing with trusts and with complaints against railroads.[28] In New York he interviewed Collis P. Huntington, one of the founders of the Southern Pacific, who appears in the novel as Shelgrim. As a result of this research, the political and economic details of *The Octopus* are like its geography. Just as Norris does not limit himself to the San Joaquin, so he does not confine himself to events of the pre-Mussel-Slough period, but rather incorporates into the novel three decades of farmer-railroad controversy and maneuvering.

Norris used his friends as models for many of his characters, though it is impossible to say whether an abstract conception of a character preceded Norris' use of an acquaintance for a prototype or whether the acquaintance was his starting point. In any case, his three central characters, Presley, Annixter, and Vanamee, are modeled more or less on himself and on his friends Seymour Waterhouse and Bruce Porter. Waterhouse, like Annixter, had a gruff, irascible temperament, while Porter shared Vanamee's mysticism. Presley is based on Norris himself in the limited sense that he often voices Norris' ideas on art, though even in this respect he is sometimes a foil for these ideas as well. But he is not, as we shall see, a sustained authorial "spokesman."

A number of important characters in *The Octopus* were suggested to Norris by participants in the Mussel Slough massacre and its aftermath. Magnus Derrick is partly based on a Major McQuiddy, the president of the farmers' organization, and Delaney on Walter Crow, a sharpshooter who was responsible for most of the deaths at the fight.[29] Dyke, the engineer-hop farmer who is twice victimized by the railroad, is based on Chris Evans, a train robber who was captured in 1893 after several years of eluding posses. Dyke, like Evans, is a farmer who becomes an outlaw after deciding that his life has been ruined by the railroad, and like Evans he is finally run down and captured.[30]

To give fictional shape to his abundant material, Norris turned most of all to Zola. He seems not to have been influenced either by earlier novels on the Mussel Slough tragedy (Josiah Royce's *The Feud of Oakfield Creek* [1887] is the best known) or by novels dealing with railroads or trusts. Rather, as is true of all of Norris' best work, the primary literary influence was Zola. He drew upon Zola for such matters as the metaphor of the railroad engine as an animal (*La Bête humaine*) and the lyric exaltation of fertility and reproduction (*La Terre* and *La Faute de l'Abbé Mouret*). He also borrowed an entire plot from Zola, that of the symbolic conquest of the grave by the "return" of a girl many years after her death in the form of a girl with the same name ("Angeline"). Most important of all, however, Norris derived from *Germinal* and *La Terre*, Zola's most successful panoramic novels, two of the unifying structural devices of *The Octopus*. *Germinal*, which deals with a dispute between miners and their employers, suggested to Norris the technique (also used in *La Terre* to a lesser degree) of introducing an outsider into an economic struggle and of using his innocence as a means both for exposition and for the gradual crystallization of an attitude toward the dispute. *La Terre*, though it covers six years, begins and ends at harvest time (like *The Octopus*) and emphasizes the universality and permanence of the cycle of nature, of the movement from birth to death to rebirth. Both *La Terre* and *The Octopus* deal with the relationship of man to this cycle, and both use the cycle as a thematic and structural core.[31] In *The Octopus*, Norris combined these two forms. Presley, an outsider in the valley, spends approximately a year there, from harvest to harvest, and during that time he reaches a conclusion about the conflict between the ranchers and the railroad which is derived from his understanding of the natural cycle of reproduction.

When Norris finished *The Octopus* in December, 1900, he attempted to find a serial publisher for it. After being turned down by several magazines, he realized that the novel was "a very difficult story to place that way,"[32] and resigned himself to book publication alone. *The Octopus* therefore appeared initially in April, 1901, published by Doubleday, Page & Company, and was the last novel by Norris to be published during his lifetime.

3

The structural and thematic center of *The Octopus* is the growth of a crop of wheat. The cycle of growth, from September to July, contains two large substructures of conflict, both of which are resolved within the forward thrust of the wheat's growth. The first substructure deals with three young men—the poet Presley, the ascetic shepherd Vanamee, and the rancher Annixter—each of whom undergoes a transformation in values and belief following a perception of the meaning of the process of growth. The second substructure is that of the struggle for the wheat by the ranchers and the railroad, each seeking the largest possible profit from its growth. I will take up these substructures individually in order to show how each contributes to the theme of man's relationship to nature.

First, however, it is important to recognize that Norris explicitly establishes the cycle of the wheat's growth as an epitome of the divine energy or force present in nature and in all natural processes. As Presley views the harvested fields toward the end of the novel, he "seemed for one instant to touch the explanation of existence." The explanation is that "FORCE only existed— FORCE that brought men into the world, FORCE that crowded them out of it to make way for the succeeding generation, FORCE that made the wheat grow, FORCE that garnered it from the soil to give place to the succeeding crop" (II, 343). This universal force inherent in the life processes of both human and nonhuman existence is finally characterized by Presley as "primordial energy flung out from the hand of the Lord God himself, immortal, calm, infinitely strong" (II, 343).

Since the wheat and its cycle of growth are objectifications of the divine, it is not surprising that two of the central characters experience what are basically religious conversions in the presence of the wheat, and that they find confirmation of their transcendentally derived truths in the cycle of the wheat's growth. Both Annixter and Vanamee are initially isolated, troubled, fundamentally selfish men—the first dominated by fear of love, the second by hate of death. Annixter's self-centered suspicion of others makes him rough, intolerant, and "widely hated." He attempts to fight off his love for Hilma Tree, a pretty milkmaid, because he fears being trapped into marriage, but is unable to do so. His clumsy attempt to kiss her and his clumsier proposal for an illicit relationship repel the girl, though she loves him, and she runs off to San Francisco. When he discovers that Hilma is gone, Annixter wanders out into the wheat fields and mulls over the problem. His "imagination, unused, unwilling machine, began to work." Realizing the selfishness of his attitude toward Hilma,

> By a supreme effort, not of the will, but of the emotion, he fought his way across that vast gulf that for a time had gaped between Hilma and the idea of his marriage. Instantly, like the swift blending of beautiful colours, like the harmony of beautiful chords of music, the two ideas melted into one, and in that moment into his harsh, unlovely world a new idea was born. Annixter stood suddenly upright, a mighty tenderness, a gentleness of spirit, such as he had never conceived of, in his heart strained, swelled, and in a moment seemed to burst. Out of the dark furrows of his soul, up from the deep rugged recesses of his being, something rose, expanding. He opened his arms wide. An immense happiness overpowered him. Actual tears came to his eyes. Without knowing why, he was not ashamed of it. This poor, crude fellow, harsh, hard, narrow, with his unlovely nature, his fierce truculency, his selfishness, his obstinacy, abruptly knew that all the sweetness of life, all the great vivifying eternal force of humanity had burst into life within him (II, 81-82).

At that moment Annixter notices the young wheat in the early morning light. Triumphantly he identifies the emergence of the

wheat with the bursting forth of his love, since both contribute to
the perpetual renewal of life.

> There it was, the Wheat, the Wheat. . . . Once more the
> strength of nations was renewed. Once more the force of the
> world was revivified. Once more the Titan, benignant, calm,
> stirred and woke, and the morning abruptly blazed into glory
> upon the spectacle of a man whose heart leaped exuberant with
> the love of a woman, and an exulting earth gleaming transcen-
> dent with the radiant magnificence of an inviolable pledge
> (II, 82-83).

When Presley encounters Vanamee at the opening of the
novel, he recalls Vanamee's tragic love many years earlier for
Angèle, who had been raped and had died in childbirth.
Vanamee's face is "stamped with an unspeakable sadness, a
deathless grief," and he is a man "whose life had suddenly
stopped at a certain moment of its development" (I, 32). In a
paroxysm of grief, he attempts to use his strange hypnotic power
of attracting others to call the dead Angèle to him. He receives a
faint "Answer," an impulse in reply, and soon haunts the mission
garden where this has occurred, striving to call forth Angèle completely. On the same spring night of Annixter's experience on the
edge of the wheat field, Vanamee, "dizzied with mysticism," his
"imagination reshaping itself," feels the "Answer" very close (II,
104). It appears, and though he learns that it is not Angèle, but
rather her daughter, he is yet exultant, "Angèle or Angèle's
daughter, it was all one with him. It was She. Death was overcome. The grave vanquished. Life, ever-renewed, alone existed.
Time was naught; change was naught; all things were immortal
but evil; all things eternal but grief" (II, 106). At this moment
he notices the wheat:

> There it was. The Wheat! The Wheat! In the night it had
> come up. . . . Once more the pendulum of the seasons swung in

129

its mighty arc, from death back to life. Life out of death, eternity rising from out dissolution. There was the lesson. Angèle was not the symbol, but the *proof* of immortality. The seed dying, rotting and corrupting in the earth; rising again in life unconquerable, and in immaculate purity—Angèle dying as she gave birth to her little daughter, life springing from her death—the pure, unconquerable, coming forth from the defiled (II, 106).

Thus, in parallel scenes each character plumbs his soul in the presence of the just-emerging wheat and each struggles through to a basic truth of existence—that love is a universal benevolent force perpetually renewing life, and that the death of the individual is inconsequential in comparison with the continuity of life on earth. The two experiences—one centering on love, the other on death—sum up the meaning of the eternal cycle of reproduction, growth, and death which man shares with all nature. On the basis of his new understanding of love, Annixter undertakes marriage in a spirit of kindness and generosity, whereas Vanamee, now accepting the transience of death, casts aside his all-absorbing grief and embraces life in the person of Angèle's daughter, with whom he is soon in love. Both are now whole men who have learned that the good life is one which transcends the narrowly selfish, and both are no longer "shunners of men" but rather are men who participate in and contribute to life. Both have seen God in nature, rather than in Bible, church, or sermon, and have experienced the reality of great religious truths by discovering that these truths are in actuality the eternal natural processes of life.

This reshaping of the supernatural into the natural is particularly clear in the case of Vanamee. Early in the novel he had explicitly rejected the consolation of the Pauline assurance that his dead Angèle had been spiritually reborn (I, 137-42). With the appearance of Angèle's daughter, however, he at last recognizes the great truth that life is eternal, whether its continuity be expressed in a new crop of wheat or in a child. At the moment of his perception of both the new crop and Angèle's daughter, he cries out the words of St. Paul, " 'Oh, Grave, where is thy victory?' " (II, 107). His exultation, however, is evolutionary rather than Christian, for he believes that Angèle's daughter is "not the symbol, but the *proof* of immortality" (II, 106). And he now uses St. Paul's seed symbolism, which he had earlier rejected, as a literal confirmation of the conquest of death by nature's eternal fecundity. Thus, to state it baldly, by means of the conversions of Annixter and Vanamee, Norris translated Christian love into propagation of the species, spiritual rebirth into persistence of the type. He found in the cycle of organic fecundity not merely a symbolic reflection of the Christian themes of love and rebirth, but the themes themselves. Finally, Norris presents each character's moment of understanding as a transcendental perception. They are religious experiences in which the individual imaginatively and emotionally plumbs his own soul and the natural world to discover divine truths.

One of the principal unifying themes in the conversions of Annixter and Vanamee is that both men at their moments of insight perceive the universality and glory of nature's fecundity, of the perpetual renewal by sexual reproduction of the means by which men live and of life itself. But when Annixter and Vanamee translate nature's revivifying power into human terms, they find confirmation not only of the magnificence of sexual reproduction but also of the distinctly human characteristic of love. It is true that an evolutionary theist could find an equivalent in nature for love, since the generosity and unselfishness conventionally attributed to love are roughly paralleled in nature by the principle which subordinates individuals to species. Indeed, Norris has Presley reach an approximation of this conclusion at the end of the novel. But, despite this theoretical parallel, human love and plant reproduction seem distant and unrelated within the concrete particulars of a novel. Norris' need, therefore, was to make emotionally convincing the idea that man can find in the changeless, eternal laws of nature the principles by which to guide his life, even though the growth of a crop of wheat seems irrelevant to human love. To achieve this effect, Norris used an interwoven pattern of imagery and symbolism. One of his central images, for example, was that of the sexual quality of the natural cycle of planting, growth, and harvest. In numerous passages describing this cycle, Norris relied on an erotic lyricism in order to suggest a similarity between the natural cycle of reproduction on the one hand and human love and its sexual expression on the other. Thus, at ploughing time,

> Deep down there in the recesses of the soil, the great heart throbbed once more, thrilling with passion, vibrating with desire, offering itself to the caress of the plough, insistent, eager, imperious. Dimly one felt the deep-seated trouble of the earth, the uneasy agitation of its members, the hidden tumult of its womb, demanding to be made fruitful, to reproduce, to disengage the eternal renascent germ of Life that stirred and struggled in its loins (I, 122).

Norris also implied an affinity between human love and nonhuman reproduction by symbolizing Hilma and Angèle's daughter as aspects of the cycle of death and rebirth in nature. Hilma's bodily fullness, her work in the dairy, and her love of the sun combine to make her a symbol of the rich fecundity of the earth by day. Angèle's daughter represents darkness, night, and the grave, for these are the contexts in which we experience her as Vanamee attempts to call her forth during his nightly vigil in the mission garden. Hilma and Angèle's daughter are thus seemingly contrasting symbols of life and death. Yet, because of the universal principle of rebirth, they are really complementary symbols of nature's fecundity. And because they are human, their fecundity is intrinsically linked with the idea of love. When Hilma becomes pregnant, "She moved surrounded by an invisible atmosphere of Love. Love was in her wide-opened brown eyes, Love . . . radiated in a faint lustre from her dark, thick hair" (II, 209). And Angèle's daughter is "reborn" into life and daylight when she and Vanamee meet as lovers in the sundrenched wheat fields.

Norris' technique in his symbolic portrayal of Hilma and Angèle's daughter was, therefore, first to suggest their relationship to the natural cycle of reproduction and then to infuse into their own "rebirth" cycle the element of love. Finally, Norris used a parallel seed imagery for both Annixter and Vanamee to describe the birth of their perception of nature's benevolence and love. The Annixter-Vanamee sections of *The Octopus* are thus pervaded by an imagery and symbolism which seek to persuade the reader that love and its accompanying virtues are inseparable from nature's fecundity, and therefore that the spirit of love is present throughout nature. This theme, however, which is of course closely related to the evolutionary theistic core of the novel, is not one that Norris demonstrates by fictional or discursive exposition. It is rather a belief which he "proves" primarily by imagery and by symbolism.

Norris, then, is a symbolic writer in a sense not usually associated with him. Marius Bewley, for example, compares Norris' symbolism in *The Octopus* unfavorably with that of earlier nineteenth-century American symbolic writers. Bewley writes:

Melville's symbols move inward, or downward, toward primordial depths of consciousness. Their meanings are not limited by the boundaries of the material world. But Norris' symbols, effective as they sometimes are within their small limits, are little more than marginal illustrations to his dramatized economics and sociology. The symbols explore nothing, discover nothing. They merely lend an obvious kind of structure and emphasis to the story and the meaning.[33]

The weakness in this criticism is not only that it presupposes that exploratory symbols are better than designatory ones (ours is an age of romantic value assumptions) but that it is based on isolated symbols in *The Octopus* and neglects the "downward" probing quality of large patterns of symbolism in the novel. For example, Angèle's daughter is a "marginally illustrative" symbol. "She is the symbol of the wheat," Norris reminded himself in the character sketches he prepared for the novel,[34] and he even portrayed her as a ripe stalk of wheat with her golden hair and "the strange, balancing movement of her head upon her slender neck" (II, 347). But in his total pattern of symbolism and imagery involving the relationship between fecundity and love in man and nature, of which Angèle's daughter is a part, Norris is reaching out toward "primordial depths of consciousness." For surely his symbolic probing of man's inexpressible sense of affinity with his natural world, and of man's faith in love as the unifying force in all life, carries the impact and meaning of his pattern beyond the "boundaries of the material world."

Presley, the third central character in *The Octopus*, also draws knowledge from the cycle of the wheat, though his process of deriving truth differs considerably from that of Annixter and Vanamee. First, his knowledge is more inclusive and less personal than theirs, and it bears more directly on the struggle between the ranchers and the railroad. Secondly, he does not acquire truth in one sharp and dramatic realization, as they do, but rather proceeds through various stages of knowledge to his final realization at the end of the novel. Finally, Presley's artistic ideas and career are somewhat independent of his progressive understanding of the wheat. There are several hazards, therefore, in regarding Presley as a static spokesman of Norris' ideas, as many critics have tried to do, since neither Presley's artistic nor his philosophical position fully represents Norris' beliefs at every point in the novel.

First, let me consider Presley as a poet. In his critical essays of 1901-1902 Norris expressed an ideal of art which had already appeared both in his characterization of Presley and in *The Octopus* as a whole. Norris believed that the best art was romantic in the sense that it strove to express vast themes which incorporated basic racial and national characteristics. But he argued that romance was not to be found in the past or in the exotic but in the commonplace realities of life, if these are explored and probed beneath their surface.[35] At the opening of *The Octopus*, Presley wishes to write a romance of the West, but he fails to realize that his vast epic can and should be written about such seemingly prosaic subjects as freight rates and tenant farmers. He fails, in other words, to write a poetic equivalent of *The Octopus*, but rather seeks his epic material in the legends of Spanish California. Later in the novel, when he becomes emotionally involved in the farmers' struggle, he moves from poetry to propaganda. His poem "The Toilers" is a "message," but it is not art, and Presley himself, despite its success, feels that he is unable to communicate with the people.[36] Both Presley's early and later failures stem from the same cause—his intellectuality. His temperament has been overrefined by his years of study, and he is either too withdrawn or too sensitive to participate successfully in the concrete actualities of life which are the artist's true matrix. Norris' anti-intellectualism thus appears in *The Octopus* in two major ways. It is present in a "positive" form when Annixter and Vanamee, both college graduates, learn that in order to grasp essential truths of existence they must discard intellect for emotion and

135

imagination. It appears in a "negative" form in Presley's over-intellectualized and therefore blocked artistic vision. There is a hint, toward the close of the novel, in Presley's response to Hilma, that with the aid of a strong woman he might, like Condy Rivers, reinforce his temperament and prove himself as an artist. Despite this suggestion, his failure as a poet is one of the major weaknesses in Norris' construction of *The Octopus*, for we are asked to credit his concluding philosophical vision after many passages in which we have learned of his incapacitating intellectuality.

Although Presley's rate of attaining truth is slower than that of Annixter and Vanamee, his method is the same. Like them, his process is one of achieving a "larger view," of casting aside personal values for a philosophical perspective. By this means Presley learns the truth of good and evil in relation to the conflict between the ranchers and the railroad, just as Annixter had learned the truth of love and Vanamee of life and death. In emphasizing the need for an enlarged, self-effacing vision if one is to perceive fundamental truths, Norris was probably drawing more upon a generic Christian attitude than upon any specific source, though this method of deriving truth is also central to evolutionary morality and is expressed by both Zola and Le Conte.[37]

At the opening of *The Octopus* Presley is characterized as an overrefined poet searching for the True Romance, an epic theme upon which to write his great poem of the West. On a slope overlooking many miles of the rich San Joaquin, he gazes out over the bare, harvested fields, seeing in their immensity "his epic, his inspiration, his West." But at this time Presley cannot grasp the meaning of the scene, and "terrible, formless shapes, vague figures . . . whirled at a gallop through his imagination" (I, 44). Moreover, he proceeds no farther, for there is a violent interruption as a crack railroad engine plows into a herd of sheep which had wandered onto a nearby track. "The inspiration vanished

like a mist," and, in the oft-repeated epithets, Presley characterizes the railroad as "the soulless Force, the iron-hearted Power,
the monster, the Colossus, the Octopus" (I, 48).

Presley is soon drawn into the wheat growers' struggle against
the railroad. Immediately after a meeting at which their league
discovers that it has been betrayed to the railroad he again perceives the wheat, this time the wheat growing in the night. He
realizes now that the process of growth is "indifferent, gigantic,
resistless," that "Men . . . were born, lived . . . died, and were forgotten; while the Wheat . . . grew steadily under the night" (II,
161). But the fight at the irrigation ditch and the death of his
friends shake Presley out of any equilibrium and comfort this
realization might have given him. Under the impact of the personal tragedies evolving from the fight, he is overcome by a "som-
bre brooding malevolence." After making an impassioned speech
attacking the railroad, he tries to kill S. Behrman, the local railroad agent.

A month later, in San Francisco, he is still full of a "spirit of
unrest and revolt." On a whim, he approaches Shelgrim, the
president of the railroad. He lectures Presley:

> "You are dealing with forces, young man, when you speak of
> Wheat and the Railroads, not with men. There is the Wheat,
> the supply. It must be carried to feed the People. There is the
> demand. The Wheat is one force, the Railroad, another, and
> there is the law that governs them—supply and demand. Men
> have only little to do in the whole business. Complications may
> arise, conditions that bear hard on the individual—crush him
> maybe—*but the Wheat will be carried to feed the people* as in-
> evitably as it will grow. If you want to fasten the blame of
> the affair at Los Muertos on any one person, you will make a
> mistake. Blame conditions, not men" (II, 285).[38]

To Presley, Shelgrim's argument "rang with the clear reverbera-
tion of truth." He now conceives of nature in terms of a "colossal

137

indifference only, a vast trend toward appointed goals. Nature was, then, a gigantic engine, a vast Cyclopean power . . ." (II, 286). But despite its "truth," Presley takes little satisfaction in this knowledge. He discovers that Shelgrim's concept of force is inadequate, that he is still concerned with individuals. "The Railroad might indeed be a force only, which no man could control and for which no man was responsible, but his friends had been killed . . ." (II, 317).

Before leaving for India, Presley returns to the San Joaquin, to the scene of his first awareness of the wheat, and again views the bare fields, the cycle of growth now completed. He now realizes "strong and true the sense and the significance of the enigma of growth," for he perceives that "Men were naught, death was naught, life was naught; FORCE only existed . . ." (II, 343). Each succeeding perception of the wheat by Presley had meant an increase in knowledge. His first perception, on this same slope, had been vague. The second, after the league meeting, ended with an awareness of the power of natural processes, the insignificance of man. This was strengthened by Shelgrim's concept of force. But Shelgrim's force was essentially negative—something to blame— and still did not quiet Presley's unrest. Each previous perception had been vitiated by events concerning individuals. But now, instead of a slaughter of sheep or a massacre at an irrigation ditch, Vanamee appears with a theory of good and evil derived from his experience with Angèle's daughter. " 'You are all broken, all cast down by what you have seen in this valley,' " he tells Presley.

> "Well, the end is not yet. What is it that remains after all is over, after the dead are buried and the hearts are broken? Look at it from the vast height of humanity—'the greatest good to the greatest numbers.' What remains? . . . Try to find that, not only in this, but in every crisis of the world's life, and you

will find, if your view be large enough, that it is *not* evil, but good, that in the end remains" (II, 344-345).

The ship on which Presley leaves for India is loaded with San Joaquin grain for the relief of an Indian famine. As Presley muses over the personal tragedies of the ranchers, he reminds himself of Vanamee's question, "What was the larger view, what contributed the greatest good to the greatest numbers" (II, 360). With this question as a guide, he now realizes that despite the pain and destruction which had so disturbed him during the course of the struggle, the wheat survives as a benevolent nourisher of men.

> But the WHEAT remained. Untouched, unassailable, undefiled, that mighty world-force, that nourisher of nations, wrapped in Nirvanic calm, indifferent to the human swarm, gigantic, resistless, moved onward in its appointed grooves. Through the welter of blood at the irrigating ditch, through the sham charity and shallow philanthropy of famine-relief committees, the great harvest of Los Muertos rolled like a flood from the Sierras to the Himalayas to feed thousands of starving scarecrows on the barren plains of India.
>
> Falseness dies; injustice and oppression in the end of everything fade and vanish away. Greed, cruelty, selfishness, and inhumanity are short-lived; the individual suffers, but the race goes on. Annixter dies, but in a far-distant corner of the world a thousand lives are saved. The larger view always and through all shams, all wickedness, discovers the Truth that will, in the end, prevail, and all things, surely, inevitably, resistlessly work together for good (II, 360-361).

It is therefore not Norris who varies between ideas of amoral force and triumphant good, as has often been charged, but rather Presley as Norris dramatized his gradual and troubled progress toward Truth. Presley's preoccupation with individual tragedy and his personal involvement hinder him from achieving the "larger view." This is his earlier, moral attitude. However, led by his second perception of the wheat and by Shelgrim, he formulates an amoral, impersonal conception of force. This too fails to answer his doubts. It is only with the return to a moral position, now on a cosmic level, that he achieves the "larger view" and Truth. The representation of any of Presley's earlier generalizations as Norris', no matter how true they seemed to Presley at the time, is false in the light of what Norris had ultimately in mind for Presley.

The way is now clear to discuss the implications of Presley's final perception for both the farmer-railroad controversy and the novel's central themes. It should be understood from the first, however, that the vital thematic conflict in the social substructure of the novel is not between the ranchers and the railroad but between the natural law of supply and demand and those who attempt to impede that law or to exploit it excessively. This larger and more inclusive conflict is more obvious in *The Pit*, in which the bulls and bears are similar, despite their opposition, because both use the need to distribute wheat as an opportunity for speculative gain. In *The Octopus*, both the ranchers and the railroad fail to heed the omnipotence and benevolence of the natural law of supply and demand which determines the production and distribution of wheat. Both groups greedily exploit the demand for wheat, the first by speculative "bonanza" farming, the second by monopoly of transportation. Norris hammers at this vital similarity early in Book II in parallel images of the ranchers and the railroad "sucking dry" the land. First, he describes a railroad map of California on which the railroad's lines are drawn in red:

> The map was white, and it seemed as if all the colour which should have gone to vivify the various counties, towns, and cities marked upon it had been absorbed by that huge, sprawling organism, with its ruddy arteries converging to a central point.

It was as though the State had been sucked white and colourless, and against this pallid background the red arteries of the monster stood out, swollen with life-blood, reaching out to infinity, gorged to bursting, an excrescence, a gigantic parasite fattening upon the life-blood of an entire commonwealth (II, 5).

The greed of the railroad, however, is matched by that of the ranchers, for

they had no love for their land. They were not attached to the soil. They worked their ranches as a quarter of a century before they had worked their mines. To husband the resources of their marvellous San Joaquin, they considered niggardly, petty, Hebraic. To get all there was out of the land, to squeeze it dry, to exhaust it, seemed their policy. When, at last, the land was worn out, would refuse to yield, they would invest their money in something else; by then, they would all have made fortunes. They did not care. "After us the deluge" (II, 14).

Both groups, moreover, engage in corrupt acts in their struggle for possession of the profitable land and its crops. There is no doubt that Norris considered the railroad trust the more culpable of the two, and that he indirectly suggested means of alleviating its hold on the community. Indeed, his frequent imagery of the railroad company as a devouring monster and the ranchers' league as a terrified but dangerous animal at bay reflects his sentiments. But these sentiments did not prevent him from symbolizing the entire dispute in its climax, in which he depicted both sides as equally responsible—or as not responsible—for the shedding of blood.[39] For Norris' primary emphasis was not on the question of responsibility for the massacre, but rather on the theme that the cycle of growth and the fulfillment of demand by supply are completed regardless of whatever harm and destruction men bring upon themselves in their attempt to hinder or manipulate these natural processes for their own profit.

Norris thus subscribed to a belief in a beneficent cosmic determinism, a belief that seems to render all human action both devoid of free will and inherently good. There is no doubt that Norris accepted the idea of the omnipotence and benevolence of the law of supply and demand. He again dramatized and discussed this law in *The Pit*, and in *The Octopus* it appears not only in Shelgrim's lecture and in Presley's final perception, but in Norris' own characterization of Shelgrim early in the novel (I, 99-100). Norris seems to have absorbed this idea from economic and social theories current in his own time, though, like his response to evolutionary theism, he accepted it as a "Big Idea" rather than as a carefully studied premise. He had taken a course in political economy at Berkeley in which the two prescribed texts were solidly in the camp of the classical school of economics —that is, both emphasized the universality of economic principles and thereby brought these principles close to natural law.[40] And he seems to have been affected by the common late-nineteenth-century practice of concluding that since natural selection was an omnipotent law of natural life, there must be similar laws in economic and social life. Ideas of economic determinism pervaded late-nineteenth-century thought, and were often used to defend the existing order. The same ideas were also Marxian, as Jack London noted in a review of *The Octopus*.[41] In any case, Norris viewed the law of supply and demand not simply as a price regulating principle in economic affairs, but as a natural law and therefore, since he was an evolutionary theist, as omnipotent and benevolent. Once it is recognized that Norris thought of the law in this way, his conception of it can be clarified by a glance back at his handling of the natural law of the survival of the fittest. In *Vandover*, this law is also both omnipotent and benevolent, yet Vandover determined his own fate by disregarding its provisions. Vandover is thus responsible for his fall, even though he is destroyed by an omnipotent, impersonal law. Norris' former history teacher at Berkeley, Thomas Bacon, recognized this basic paradox in Norris' thinking. Norris, he wrote in early 1903, "knew two things: first, that the individual has self-sovereignty; second, that the universe is run by law, a law which is absolutely certain, and which takes up into itself and uses for its own ends the aberrations of the human will."[42]

We now return to Shelgrim's argument that the railroad cannot be blamed for its activities, since it is a product of the ungovernable demand for transportation. With Norris' idea of moral responsibility within natural law in mind, one can see that Shelgrim's defense is contravened in the novel in two major ways, despite the fact that Presley finds this defense convincing. First, the punishment of Behrman, the railroad's principal agent, suggests that man is responsible for any evil acts he may commit while participating in the fulfillment of natural law. Norris here implies that those who exploit a demand for "all the traffic will bear" must bear the responsibility for the pain and harm they cause. Secondly, Cedarquist's call for an aroused public to curb the excesses of the trust assumes that such acts can be controlled to permit natural law to operate more efficiently and with greater benefit. Norris attributes to the railroad a conventional defense of its malpractices (used by both Jay Gould and Leland Stanford)[43] in order to demonstrate the falsity of that defense. Although Norris would accept Shelgrim's argument that those who grow or ship wheat are parallel agents within the inevitable functioning of the law of supply and demand, he would deny Shelgrim's plea that individual farmers and individual railroads are not responsible for the way in which they perform their roles. Presley is taken in by Shelgrim's defense because he has an incomplete awareness at that point of both the relations of individuals to natural laws and the essential benevolence of such laws. By the close of the novel, however, Presley at last realizes

143

that though individual evil and its consequences exist within the functioning of the natural law of supply and demand, that law is ultimately beneficial to the mass of men. The famine-relieving crop of wheat concretely proves the utilitarian morality ("the greatest good," etc.) of the law determining the production of the crop. And that law, like all natural laws, is characterized by divine immanence.

In both substructures of the novel, then, the wheat functions as the objectification of divine force or energy, as God immanent, apprehendable, eternal, omnipotent, and benevolent, whether that force is expressed in the wheat itself, in the cycle of its growth, or in the law controlling its production. The wheat and its processes thus embody a moral norm, and, as in most religious systems, man may choose to recognize and obey the truths there embodied or to hazard neglect of or opposition to them. It is at this point that the two substructures of the novel unite. Man can derive great truths from the wheat, as do Annixter and Vanamee, and ally himself with its processes by accepting ideas of love and death which transcend the self. Or he can oppose himself to its lessons through selfishness, blindness, or greed, as do the ranchers and the railroad. God is good and God is omnipotent, but man must choose for himself whether to know and obey God and thereby receive God-given benefits.

The wheat as the moral center of *The Octopus* is nowhere more apparent than in the scene toward the close of the novel in which it destroys S. Behrman. This incident is often justly criticized for its melodrama; yet its melodrama is the key to its significance, since the explicit presentation of divine vengeance is almost inevitably melodramatic. For the last time Norris gives the supernatural concrete objectification, as the heavenly admonition that "vengeance is mine" is in Behrman's death obeyed to the letter. Behrman has escaped chastisement at the hands of men and is left to the wheat. Like the evolutionary theists, Norris affirms the reality and immediacy of the moral order immanent in nature, though he goes beyond them in his eagerness to demonstrate dramatically that traditional religious beliefs are functionally operative in the processes of nature rather than promised now and redeemable hereafter.

The Octopus is Norris' fullest and most elaborate attempt to translate the conventionally supernatural into the natural. The novel above all seeks to dramatize the validity of such traditional paradoxes as the coexistence of free will and determinism, the eternity of life despite death, and the emergence of good out of evil. Norris' involvement in the effort to revitalize the traditional paradoxes of religious faith is one of the primary sources of the novel's depth and intensity. But the same paradoxes are also responsible for much that is least successful in *The Octopus*. Most obviously, they lead to naive and ludicrous effects when the conventionally supernatural is translated too literally into the natural, as in the death of Behrman. More vitally, they cause a discrepancy between the novel's themes and its concrete world. For one of the few certainties about religious paradoxes is that they are against the evidence—that life either contradicts them or offers no support for them. This is why they are *religious* paradoxes; they demand faith and the suspension of our "common-sense" estimation of their possible truth. They are founded in man's desire and need to believe in both free will and a cosmic moral order, in life after death, and in the inevitable triumph of good, even though the evidence of the senses is against the truth of these beliefs. But the world of the novel is a world of "the evidence of the senses," of men in concrete personal and social contexts in which experience proves that there is no order unless men themselves create it, that death is real and permanent, and that evil often flourishes and goes unpunished. In *The Octopus* we are asked to accept Vanamee's celebration of death after he has mourned the death of Angèle for sixteen years, and Presley's affirmation of moral order after he has experienced the chaos of the irrigation ditch and the death of his friends. To some degree, we can accept these beliefs, because they are logically consistent within the religious core of the novel. But emotionally they lack validity. Despite Norris' creation of such "concrete" evidence as Angèle's daughter and the famine-relieving crop of wheat, we are still involved in the more compelling emotional realities of Vanamee's despair and the death of Annixter. Norris not only gives these realities greater weight by sheer length and detail of attention, but he also sacrifices conviction for dramatic surprise by his *deus-ex-machina* introduction of Angèle's daughter and the crop of wheat. Much of the criticism of *The Octopus* as intellectually or philosophically muddled has been misdirected. There is very little that is muddled in Norris' central themes. They are consistent within his evolutionary theism, whatever one may think of that system. Where Norris goes astray is in failing to make these themes emotionally convincing as well as logically consistent.

It might be argued that if Presley's final conclusion seems unconvincing, as though it were "against the evidence," such an effect is apt, since the idea of a triumphant moral order is of this nature. But the function of art when it presents themes transcending experience is to move us sufficiently to suspend our disbelief and to accept the possibility of the truth of these themes—indeed, even to move us sufficiently to infuse these themes into our lives and so create their truth. This task is particularly difficult in fiction, however, since by its very nature the novel deals more with social and human probabilities than with religious possibilities. Only the greatest novelists, a Hawthorne or a Dostoevski, have succeeded in making religious themes the central matter of

146

their novels. And even they have relied on the supernatural and the strange, while Norris attempts to keep *The Octopus* within the probabilities of his late-nineteenth-century American scene. In all, the evaluation of Norris' work by many critics, that *McTeague* is the better novel and *The Octopus* the more profound and stimulating, is correct. The explanation of this difference resides in the critical commonplace that in art, and particularly in fiction, evil and the fall of man are more easily and convincingly portrayed than their opposites, and that Norris' career had taken him from the tragic possibilities of man's animal nature to a natural world glorified by God's presence and by man's ability to know and to profit by that presence.

In this discussion of the religious core of *The Octopus*, I have not considered fully enough either the prominence Norris gives to the problems raised by modern industrialism or the relationship of these problems to the novel's religious themes. Much that is central in Norris' social ideas can be explained by examining his machine imagery and symbolism in the novel. It has sometimes been held that in *The Octopus* Norris reveals a traditional romantic distrust of the machine and of industrialism.[44] Superficially, he does seem to be in this tradition. He frequently gives the railroad a "death" imagery in contrast to the "life" imagery of the wheat and the earth,[45] and in such symbolic incidents as the massacre of the sheep or Hilma's miscarriage he depicts the railroad as a destroyer of nature's fecundity. The symbolic meaning of the railroad engine throughout *The Octopus*, however, is conditioned more by the theme of the novel than by a conventional romanticism. Individual engines, such as that which destroys the flock of sheep, do not symbolize the machine as a power antithetical to nature. Rather they symbolize a particular railroad company whose practices are antithetical to a particular natural law. Norris introduces this symbolism at the close of the passage describing the sheep massacre:

> Then, faint and prolonged, across the levels of the ranch, he heard the engine whistling for Bonneville. Again and again, at rapid intervals in its flying course, it whistled for road crossings, for sharp curves, for trestles; ominous notes, hoarse, bellowing, ringing with the accents of menace and defiance; and abruptly Presley saw again, in his imagination, the galloping monster, the terror of steel and steam, with its single eye, Cyclopean, red, shooting from horizon to horizon; but saw it now as the symbol of a vast power, huge, terrible, flinging the echo of its thunder over all the reaches of the valley, leaving blood and destruction in its path; the leviathan, with tentacles of steel clutching into the soil, the soulless Force, the iron-hearted Power, the monster, the Colossus, the Octopus (I, 48).

The engine, then, is above all a symbol of the Octopus—that is, of the Trust. The monopoly is the soulless Force whose practices, spreading death and destruction, are opposed to the land ("tentacles of steel clutching into the soil"). Norris desires to engage our emotions to fear and hate trusts, not industrialism or the machine. His theme is not the traditional conflict between technology and nature, but rather the alliance of technology and nature in the forward thrust toward human betterment. He illustrates this alliance by means of Cedarquist, the San Francisco industrialist and shipbuilder who acts as the spokesman for Norris' social ideas. Early in Book II Cedarquist outlines to Magnus Derrick a plan whereby the producers and distributors of wheat can use the law of supply and demand in a way which benefits both themselves and mankind. He explains:

> "The great word of this nineteenth century has been Production. The great word of the twentieth century will be . . . Markets. As a market for our Production—or let me take a concrete example—as a market for our *Wheat*, Europe is played out.

Population in Europe is not increasing fast enough to keep up with the rapidity of our production. In some cases, as in France, the population is stationary. We, however, have gone on producing wheat at a tremendous rate. The result is overproduction. We supply more than Europe can eat, and down go the prices. The remedy is *not* in the curtailing of our wheat areas, but in this, we *must have new markets, greater markets.* For years we have been sending our wheat from East to West, from California to Europe. But the time will come when we must send it from West to East. . . . I mean, we must look to China. Rice in China is losing its nutritive quality. The Asiatics, though, must be fed; if not on rice, then on wheat. . . . What fatuous neglect of opportunity to continue to deluge Europe with our surplus food when the East trembles upon the verge of starvation!" (II, 21-22).[46]

On the basis of this perception, Cedarquist begins to ship wheat to the East. In short, the "mechanical" distributor of wheat (a railroad or a shipping company) can with profit to itself aid the fulfillment of a benevolent natural law rather than hinder the operation of that law by striving for excessive gain. Norris establishes a conflict not between nature and the machine but between accommodation to nature and opposition to it (or, in moral terms, between love and selfishness), and those who use the land and those who use machines can behave in either way.

Perhaps the best way to understand Norris' treatment of nature and the machine is to recognize the relationship between such concrete symbols as the wheat and the railroad engine on the one hand and such large cultural ideals as primitivism and industrial progress on the other. Norris was able to support both of these ideals without a sense of contradiction. He is like the Kipling of *Captains Courageous,* who celebrated both a boy's "education" off the Grand Banks and the father's brilliant railroad journey. He reflects the perennial capacity of the popular mind to hold

in solution the ideals of primitive simplicity and those of mechanical complexity, just as most eighteenth-century Englishmen
(as Lois Whitney has pointed out)[47] called for both a return
to the simple and a progress toward the complex, and just as the
average American feels no discrepancy in taking a jet to "get away
from it all" in the north woods.

Yet, though Norris does not distrust machines, he does distrust monopolies, and he therefore draws upon the conventional
romantic imagery of the destructive machine in order to add
emotional intensity to his engine-Octopus-Trust symbolism. The
machine as destroyer serves Norris as a reservoir of affective
imagery, as it does most nineteenth-century novelists, though it is
not a thematic key to *The Octopus*. For example, Norris in several passages portrayed nature itself as little more than a destructive machine. In one such passage, he wished to depict how
the omnipotent and impersonal power of nature appears to a
timid, withdrawn, and frightened person, one whose timidity
and whose lack of the "larger view" prevent her from sensing
the fundamental benevolence of this power. To Mrs. Derrick,
both the railroad and nature are equally destructive because of
their power. She first imagines the railroad (repeating Presley's
imagery) as a "galloping terror of steam and steel, with its single
eye, Cyclopean, red" etc. Then follows her conception of nature:

> She recognized the colossal indifference of nature, not hostile,
> even kindly and friendly, so long as the human ant-swarm was
> submissive, working with it, hurrying along at its side in the
> mysterious march of the centuries. Let, however, the insect
> rebel, strive to make head against the power of this nature, and
> at once it became relentless, a gigantic engine, a vast power,
> huge, terrible; a leviathan with a heart of steel, knowing no
> compunction, no forgiveness, no tolerance; crushing out the
> human atom with soundless calm, the agony of destruction

sending never a jar, never the faintest tremor through all that
prodigious mechanism of wheels and cogs (I, 174).

It is apparent that Norris draws upon machine imagery to provide emotional intensity to the description of any destructive
force, including nature when it is so conceived. He had portrayed
nature in this way as early as *Vandover*, which suggests a fundamental link in Norris' mind between the idea of power and the
imagery of the machine. In *The Octopus* this link was reinforced
by the obvious connection between a monopolistic railroad company and a destructive engine. The imagery of destructive machines therefore pervades *The Octopus* and seems to strengthen
the novel's themes. In fact, however, this imagery blurs the
novel's central ideas in two important ways. Norris wished to as-
sert that both the ranchers and the railroad were flawed in their
roles, and also that there was no inherent conflict between the
machine and the land. Yet the emotional meaning of the over-
powering destructive machine imagery throughout the novel—
an imagery which Norris used authoritatively as well as dramatically—is that the railroad company is the only villain and that
the machine is intrinsically evil. Thus, Norris sacrificed thematic
clarity for the melodramatic appeal of the dastardly railroad company with its infernal machine.

One of the difficulties in analyzing the social theme of *The
Octopus* is that it functions on two levels. On the cosmic level,
Norris affirms that natural laws operate despite personal and social evil, that the wheat gets through and feeds the people despite
unjust freight rates, broken promises, and corrupt politics. On
this level, in which cosmic law insures the punishment of evil and
the triumph of good, there seems little need to concern ourselves
with unjust rates or with an S. Behrman. Norris' distinction between cosmic law and individual free will, however, is present in
the novel's social as well as religious themes. He shares the late-

nineteenth-century American ability to believe that the world is constantly improving yet to view the particulars of social evil with increasing intolerance. To Norris, the optimistic moral determinism of Presley's final insight would not obviate either the reality of injustice or the need to correct it. Thousands of starving Indians may indeed be saved by San Joaquin wheat, but Norris notes at the close of *The Octopus* that the railroad's candidate, Lyman Derrick, is the Republican nominee for governor of California.

The Octopus therefore embodies a faith in moral and social progress, but it also contains a full portrayal of some of the principal social problems and injustices caused by the growth of corporate wealth and power. Three of the novel's characters play major roles in this portrait. The story of Dyke, who is discharged by the railroad after many years of faithful service and who is then ruined as a farmer by the railroad's juggling of freight rates, is a parable of the defeat of the American dream by monopolistic power. He is the honest, hardworking employee and farmer who ought to rise in the world. Instead, he is driven to vengeance by the railroad and becomes a train robber. In Dyke's fall, and also in Presley's attempt to murder S. Behrman, Norris dramatized the end-of-the-century dread of anarchism. Norris attacks the use of violence as a means of redressing oppression, but he also warns that violence will erupt if no other avenue is open.

Magnus Derrick and his son Harran are more complex portraits than Dyke. Magnus is a man of honor and conscience who has always had both the strength and the ambition to lead men. But he now finds that if he is to fight the trust, he must adopt the methods of his opponent, so strong and unscrupulous is his adversary. No longer can the man of integrity fight injustice and remain unsullied. Harran, on the other hand, is of a younger generation. For him, unlike Magnus, there is nothing incongruous in using the railroad's means so long as they can be used successfully. In Magnus and Harran, Norris illustrated the loss of personal morality caused by the intolerable pressures of corporate immorality, with the older generation tortured by the loss and the younger not even aware that it is gone.

All opposition to the railroad fails, from legal action to political corruption and violence. And though Cedarquist calls for the arousing of public opinion as a means of curbing the power of the trust, he himself acknowledges the indifference of the majority of the people, and his call is set in the context of the trivialities of the San Francisco Million-Dollar Fair and Flower Festival. In short, Norris' depiction of the realities of the dilemma posed by corporate power is neither facile nor optimistic. It encompasses a portrait of modern society in which unassailable corporate bodies wield massive strength, in which the individual is helpless in the face of this strength, and in which a lethargic public seems the only recourse to justice. Norris' description of these social realities suggests that the quality of mind underlying his cosmic optimism was not a weak-tempered need for some kind of moral affirmation, no matter how superficially founded. Norris had a full awareness of human fallibility, whether expressed in a self-deceiving Vandover or in a corporation's greed. He did not believe that "whatever is, is right" or that the world was a jolly place because "it would all work out in the end." Rather, he had a profound faith in the existence of a moral order within the total pattern of life, a faith which blunted neither his recognition of evil nor his belief that it must be opposed.

The principal social and religious themes of *The Octopus* are relevant today. Although trusts no longer plague us as they once did, many of our social problems still arise out of the relationship between the individual and vast corporate and state powers which seem inexorably to control his life. And we are still trying to find confirmation of traditional Christian and humanistic values in the dynamics of life as we know it, for increasingly we share Vanamee's belief that "There is only life." We have not successfully confronted either of these two great dilemmas of twentieth-century life, and we should therefore perhaps not deal too harshly with Norris' failings. Rather we can praise his penetrating recognition of some of the central issues of modern life, and we can admire his willingness to come to grips with them—to face the elemental problems of his age and to attempt to define them and to indicate how they might be solved. For though Angèle's daughter is unconvincing as a symbol of the continuity of life, and though Cedarquist's approach to social injustice is vague, there is little doubt that we more and more seek our moral values in "only life," and that only in a massed public voice have we found a counterbalance to huge state and corporate masses.

4

The Octopus and *McTeague* are similar in form in enough important ways to suggest, since they are also Norris' most successful novels, that he worked best within this particular structure. Each is divided into three primary narratives which are tightly interwoven in plot and theme. Each is set within a vividly described, constantly reappearing social and physical world. And each has an easily grasped central pattern of action (the fall of McTeague, the growth of a crop of wheat) which shapes and controls the entire novel and which also supplies its primary symbol. The two works differ principally in scope—from a street to a large farming district, from the fall of one man to the defeat of a valley, from man's animal past to all nature and man's place in it.

The Octopus AND The Pit

The Octopus is similar to *McTeague* in basic architectonics with one important exception, which becomes apparent when one compares the circular patterns present in both works. Mc-Teague returns to the primitive world of his Sierra boyhood at the end of the novel, and Presley returns to the San Joaquin at the close of *The Octopus* and gazes out over the harvested fields he had viewed in its opening chapter. But Presley's return coincides with the end of the wheat's cycle of growth, and his response to the fields in this final scene not only differs from his initial perception but also bears on his personal development and on the conflict between the ranchers and the railroad. In short, the distinguishing characteristic of the form of *The Octopus* is Norris' brilliant construction of the novel upon the cycle of growth. The cycle has three major phases—harvest and ploughing, emergence, and harvest—each of which plays a major role in the development of the three principal characters and in the progress of the conflict for the land. It is in relation to the wheat's cycle of growth that the novel's characters define themselves, whether learning from it or struggling for it, and it is from the cycle that the novel's theme emerges. Moreover, the process of growth structures the novel's pace. As the wheat nears the end of its cycle, the conflict over it increases in intensity and tempo, until at last harvest and armed struggle occur simultaneously.

On the whole, Norris is remarkably successful in using the concrete moments of the cycle—that is, the detailed physical realities of farming wheat—as the central source of the novel's narrative, theme, and symbolism. The wheat is not an abstraction in *The Octopus*. It lives as something planted, growing, and harvested, and when Annixter wanders out into his fields or when Presley views the bare San Joaquin, the Wheat as symbol has cogency and immediacy. Of course, given the range and complexity of Norris' attempt to build his novel upon the cycle of growth, it is not surprising that he occasionally falters. His greatest difficulty stems from the fact that the personal development of Annixter and Vanamee ends early in Book II when they experience their parallel realizations of the meaning of fecundity. Vanamee, who has no role in the novel's social substructure, then drops out of sight until its close. In other words, Norris' use of a double substructure based upon a natural cycle forced him to place certain climactic moments early in the cycle and to leave the characters involved in these events "occupationless" afterward. The early maturation of Annixter involved Norris in a somewhat analogous difficulty. Annixter is the only major character who plays an important role in both substructures. (Presley is primarily an observer of the social conflict rather than a participant.) He quickly achieves a state of personal equanimity and kindness after his vision in the wheat fields, yet he continues to take part in the ranchers' illegal and finally violent affairs. Norris tries in several ways to link Annixter's internal and external worlds, his personal conversion and his social action, but in general does not succeed, and we have the sense of a fictional dilemma which Norris was unable to resolve. For the most part, however, the wheat in *The Octopus* is like Melville's whale and Hawthorne's scarlet letter—a successfully sustained organic symbol which serves as the heart of the novel's narrative, characterization, and theme. Moreover, Norris' use of the cycle of growth as the structural center of his novel is an exciting example of how a scientific idea—here that of evolution—can influence not only the theme and subject matter of a novel but also its form. *The Octopus* is one of the few late-nineteenth-century American novels in which that age's principal scientific idea had an impact on form, unlike the widespread influence of psychological ideas on the form of the modern novel.

The Octopus is also one of the few American novels of its period to depict society with some attempt at an epic range and complexity. Norris included a map and a list of characters as introductory matter to the novel, and we very quickly become aware of his firm control and full use of the geographical and social world of the Mussel Slough district. Indeed, except for the absence of the Faulknerian dimension of time, Norris' world of Bonneville and Guadalajara, of Los Muertos and Quien Sabe, has much the same recurring, interwoven texture as Yoknapatawpha County. The size of the district, with San Francisco somewhat like Faulkner's Memphis, encouraged Norris to use the journey as a basic narrative device. In chapter after chapter, and particularly in Book I, his technique is to follow a character's movements for the day, and by means of his encounters and experiences introduce the complex strands of plot and theme that make up the novel. As Zola does in *Germinal,* Norris begins with a long section in which his "outsider" character covers almost the entire geographical and social range of the novel. ("Evidently it had been decreed that Presley should be stopped at every point of his ride that day," Norris wrote somewhat guiltily at one point in chapter I [I, 14].) Frequently Norris shifts his point of view among several characters within one journey chapter. That is, Presley will meet Annixter, and after they part Norris will follow Annixter rather than Presley. This device allowed him fluidity within his journey pattern. On the whole, despite some awkwardness here and there, Norris' technique of the journey in *The Octopus* is one of the most successful technical achievements of his career.

It was probably Norris' need to solve the difficult structural problems posed by *The Octopus* that stimulated his interest in what he called the "mechanics of fiction." In his essays of 1901-1902 he frequently commented on fictional construction, and particularly on climactic effects.[48] The novel, he argued, should begin leisurely, with its principal direction not fully apparent. Themes which at first are only casually introduced should gradually assume greater and greater importance, until at last they dominate the novel and bring it to a swift, exciting climax. In *The Octopus* Norris used this form of construction principally in relation to the fight at the irrigation ditch. At first the dispute between the ranchers and the railroad is primarily over freight rates, with the railroad's possible regrading of the land only a minor concern. But slowly the land problem becomes the central issue, until finally it erupts in violence. Norris handles the gradual increase in tension so well, however, and infuses so much emotion into the fight at the ditch, that the 130 or so pages after the fight are distinctly anticlimactic. In addition, these closing chapters contain much thematic and narrative tidying up, most of it occurring in San Francisco, which lends the entire section an overschematized, remote effect. Much of the adverse criticism of *The Octopus* has centered on material in this final portion of the novel—on Shelgrim's lecture, for example, or on Behrman's death, Mrs. Hooven's *via dolorosa*, and Presley's concluding insight. One suspects that a good deal of this frequently just criticism stems from both the novelist's and the critic's impatience with an extremely long novel after its dramatic climax.

Norris' critical writing, however, often oversimplifies his literary practice. He fails to mention in his criticism one of his most successful techniques in *The Octopus*, that of fictional economy and density, of his ability to use a character or incident in a variety of ways. The minor character Delaney, for example, appears in a remarkable number of different contexts, but always in the general role of opposition to the ranchers. Similarly, the sheep massacre incident in chapter I not only disturbs Presley's dream of a romantic epic and introduces the theme of the railroad's destructive power—its primary uses—but also results in both Vanamee and Delaney losing their jobs. Norris' expert control of this technique of multilevel repetition of incident and character is one of the major reasons the novel creates a sense of "thickness"—an impression of the concentric rather than linear effect of action and of the interwoven pattern of experience. It is remarkable how few errors Norris made in his exceedingly complex character and incident patterns. Perhaps the only major lapse of this kind is his loose handling of time in Book II, when his need to crowd a great many events into the harvest season results in some dubious chronology.[49]

Although *The Octopus* reveals important advances in Norris' technical facility, it also contains some of his usual weaknesses. Again, as in *McTeague* and *Vandover*, he is tempted by the dramatic and emotional possibilities of a symbol to overdevelop it. In *The Octopus*, so excessively does he symbolize the railroad as a devouring, destructive monster that we tend both to overidentify the symbol with his own position and to lose sight of the wheat's more central symbolic role. Moreover, the repetitious heavy rhetoric of the railroad symbolism frequently slips over into the ludicrous.

The Octopus also contains liberal quantities of sentimentalism and melodrama, two permanent ingredients of Norris' fiction. His description of Mrs. Hooven's death has occasionally had its defenders, but no one, I believe, has stood up for his depiction of Dyke's attachment to his daughter, the "little tad." As far as melodrama is concerned, however, a distinction should be made between artificial and stilted striving for effect and violent or sensational action which embodies an emotion appropriate to the moment. The first is illustrated by the close of the barn dance scene. Magnus Derrick must decide whether to join the league as its president or to remain aloof from what he knows have been its corrupt methods. As the ranchers crowd around him urging him to sign their declaration, Mrs. Derrick, who opposes his participation, enters in order to persuade him not to join. The scene reaches an overblown tableau climax as Magnus stands hesitant between the ranchers and his wife. But in such incidents as Dyke's wild escape in a railroad engine, or Magnus' confession that he is a briber, or, indeed, in the massacre scene itself, Norris avoids weak melodrama by his excellent control of the inherent excitement or pathos of a violent, sensational moment, and thereby achieves some of his most notable fictional effects.

Perhaps the most important flaw in *The Octopus* is the Vanamee plot. Its weakness is not that it is "pure romance," as Norris called it,[50] or that it is allegorical. He had handled the allegorical and improbable with some success in the Zerkow-Maria subplot of *McTeague*. His failure rather derives partly from his disregard for the fictional principle that the more improbable the event the more "logical" and "factual" must be the sequence of events leading up to it. We might accept Vanamee's strange power, but we cannot accept the fact that he had visited the mission many times in the sixteen years since Angèle's death and had remained unaware that her daughter lived close by. In addition, the Vanamee plot is too abstract and overformalized. From Angèle's rape by "The Other" to Angèle's daughter's appearance as the symbol of rebirth the entire plot is a stilted, overplain gloss on the action outside it. We are perhaps thankful for the gloss, but, as with most explication, we find it rather tedious and lifeless.

With the exception of the Vanamee plot, the basic tone of *The Octopus* is the product of a combination of the massive and the particular, the grandiose and the starkly plain. Norris' inspiration for this quality was the epic, particularly as found in Zola's later Rougon-Macquart novels and in Homer. (Both

Presley's interest in a Homeric epic of the West and Norris' self-conscious use of the Homeric kenning suggest the second parallel.) Much of the distinctive effect of *The Octopus* derives from Norris' interweaving of the "large" and the "small." Most obviously this effect dominates the novel in the sense that a vast, epic theme emerges out of the particulars of commonplace individual lives and, as Presley comes to realize, out of freight rates and land prices. It arises, too, from Norris' conscious juxtaposition of large-scale scenes (the barn dance, the rabbit drive, the protest meeting) with their "public" emotions and the feelings of individual characters within them. It is even present in his prose style, as he moves from the rich lyricism of the wheat passages to the superbly controlled simplicity of the climactic fight.

As early as the "set" scenes of *Vandover*, Norris had revealed an ability to involve the reader in the bustle, tensions, and moods of large groups. But in *The Octopus* he created for the first time individual characters whose emotions not only interest but also move us. There are several reasons for this difference. One of the most obvious is that whereas in *Vandover* and *McTeague* Norris focused directly and for the most part objectively on his tragic figures, in *The Octopus* we often know Annixter and Magnus Derrick through Presley's sympathetic response to them. The primary cause of this difference, however, is less the result of a change in Norris' fictional technique than of his enlarged sense of the complexities of character. Vandover and McTeague are conceived along "straight" lines—that is, they have heavily accentuated flaws which make them successful dramatic figures but which do not encourage identification with them. Magnus and Annixter are much richer characters. Magnus is torn between his desire and duty to lead and his repugnance for the methods he must use as a leader. But he is also motivated by his old-time gambler's instinct, by his response to his wife's pleas, and by his respect for his son Harran, who is wholeheartedly for action. Similarly Annixter's conflict over Hilma is not simply Vandover and McTeague's struggle between "pure" love and "impure" desire (though this theme is present), but is more a complex and sympathetic portrait of a man unconsciously fighting his own generous nature. These are full, "round" characters, and *The Octopus* is a lasting work not only because its themes remain relevant, but because these themes are embodied in a compelling narrative and in human beings closely observed and successfully portrayed.

5

One of the ironies of Norris' career is that it ended on a low note. Although *The Pit* was much praised on its appearance, it is today ranked far below *McTeague* and *The Octopus*, and it has occasionally been used to demonstrate the permanent immaturity of Norris' mind and art. Whatever the causes of Norris' decline in his last novel, his falling off cannot be attributed to any significant change in his method of preparation and composition. As with *The Octopus*, he centered initially on a sensational public event whose background he carefully researched and whose fictional possibilities he developed with the aid of literary borrowings and personal recollection.

He began with the world-famous corner in wheat engineered by Joseph Leiter on the Chicago exchange during 1897-98.[51] Norris spent two months in Chicago in the spring of 1901 studying newspaper accounts of Leiter's exploit and observing the operation of the Chicago Board of Trade. He also refamiliarized himself with the city (though born in Chicago he had left it as a child) and took careful notes on buildings which he planned to use as key settings.[52] Norris preserved much of Leiter's corner in

The Pit not only because its details were useful but also because its general outline supported his belief in the omnipotence of natural law. Leiter had successfully cornered the market, but his corner was disastrously broken in June, 1898, by the appearance of immense supplies of wheat which high prices had encouraged. Norris' principal changes were to reduce the length of the corner from over a year to three months, to eliminate the Spanish-American War as a factor, and to subordinate the role of rival speculators in Leiter's collapse. Despite his immersion in wheat trading affairs, however, Norris—who had repeatedly failed mathematics in college—was often at sea when faced with the need to present complex financial dealings in detail. He therefore depended on a number of experts in such matters. The most important of these, George D. Moulson—a financial reporter for the *New York Sun*—checked each chapter of the novel as it was written.

Leiter's corner supplied Norris with an obvious narrative center—the rise and fall of a financial giant. But though *The Pit* is not nearly so complex as *The Octopus*, it contains much more than this core narrative. For these additional elements of plot and structure Norris borrowed liberally from Zola's two financial novels—*La Curée* and *L'Argent*—and from Harold Frederic's *The Market Place*. Of these, the first is perhaps the most important. The plot of *La Curée* involves a triangle in which a real-estate speculator neglects his young wife for business and she in turn finds solace in a sophisticated young man who shares her interests. *L'Argent* continues to study the career of Saccard, the unscrupulous speculator of *La Curée*, but now on the Paris Bourse. Norris borrowed from this novel very little of its plot but much of its emphasis on speculation as an uncontrollable vice which grips men as though it were a feverish disease. He was also probably influenced by its climactic scene, in which a great financial structure collapses. Frederic's novel affected primarily Norris' depiction of Curtis Jadwin, the speculator protagonist of *The Pit*. Saccard is a contemptible figure, and Leiter was a Harvard-educated young man whose personal elegance was incompatible with Norris' belief that wheat trading was a brutal confrontation of bulls and bears. *The Market Place*, however, contains a full portrait of the financier as heroic conqueror—as a man who succeeds because he is stronger and more ruthless than his opponents. Moreover, Frederic's novel also has a love-business triangle. The financier wins the upper-class girl because she finds his "raw power" more appealing than the refinements of his more highly bred rival. Norris was attracted by the idea of the financier as a strong-willed fighter because it confirmed his belief in the romance beneath the commonplaces of modern life (he held that if Richard the Lionhearted were reborn it would be as a modern industrialist)[53] and because it permitted him to introduce a heroic quality into the novel by pitting the wheat against a strong opponent.

As he had done in *The Octopus*, Norris used actual persons to help construct his major characters. His father had been a self-made, wealthy Chicago businessman, and not surprisingly Norris used many of his characteristics in portraying Curtis Jadwin. Laura Jadwin shares his mother's New England background, her love of the stage, and her histrionic temperament. For Sheldon Corthell, Norris again used Bruce Porter, though this time he drew upon Porter's interest in stained glass rather than his mysticism.[54] Norris' use of his parents in *The Pit* has encouraged some rather crude Freudian readings of the novel, including one in which Norris is interpreted as Corthell and therefore is his mother's lover.[55] Such readings usually ignore much conflicting biographical evidence—that Norris' artistic ideals and practices were the opposite of Corthell's, for example, or that Norris projected much of his own fear of gambling into Jadwin's speculative

fervor. There probably are Freudian implications in *The Pit*—
and indeed in all of Norris' work—but they are neither superficially apparent nor are they adequate substitutions for a reading
of the more immediate themes of the novel.

The love plot of *The Pit* is generally singled out as the novel's
central flaw. Since it is also an aspect of the work which seems unrelated to the wheat theme, it has been suggested that it was
not part of Norris' original conception of the novel but was
rather included as a concession to public taste or editorial demand.[56] *The Octopus*, however, confirms that Norris' practice
in his trilogy was to combine personal love stories (Annixter's and
Vanamee's in that novel) with a far-reaching public event. If
he had any doubts about the possibility of continuing this practice in a novel of business life, Zola and Frederic revealed the plot
machinery by which it might be accomplished. Indeed, Norris
decided very early that Laura would be his central figure. He apparently intended to use her as he had used Presley in *The Octopus*, as a character whose flawed understanding and personal
weaknesses would serve as the principal narrative focus out of
which the novel's central themes would emerge. In November,
1901, very early in the composition of *The Pit*, he wrote I. F.
Marcosson that:

> The story is told through Laura Dearborn. *She occupies the
> center of the stage all the time*, and I shall try to interest the
> reader more in the problem of her character and career than in
> any other human element in the book. The two main themes,
> consequently, are the story of Jadwin's corner in May wheat
> and the story of his wife's "affair" with Corthell.[57]

If the love plot is the major weakness in *The Pit*, it is because of
the inadequacies of that plot, not because it was welded onto the
wheat plot at an advanced stage of the novel's conception or composition.

After about nine months of writing, Norris completed *The Pit* in June, 1902. It was accepted by the *Saturday Evening Post,* appearing in that journal from September, 1902, to January, 1903, and was then published by Doubleday, Page in February, 1903. The *Post* printed a cut version which omitted many descriptive passages as well as a major portion of the "Conclusion." In the Doubleday, Page version the novel ends with an indication that Laura has confessed to Jadwin that she almost succumbed to Corthell. Jadwin, however, says that they are both to blame, and the novel closes on a *Paradise Lost* note of the two facing a new world reunited by their mutual forgiveness and love. The *Post* omits both Laura's confession and Jadwin's forgiveness. Norris died in October, 1902, before the appearance of either closing section. There seems little doubt, however, that the published book represents his text and that the *Post* version was heavily cut by the magazine's editors in order to shorten the novel.

The Pit was Norris' most popular book, its success stimulated both by the *Post* serialization and by the "human interest" appeal of his tragic death. It also owed much of its popularity to its love triangle plot and to its exciting account of Jadwin's corner. Many of the crucial moments in both the love and business plots have a theatrical quality—that is, they are moments of high tension in drawing rooms or business offices or on the floor of the wheat exchange. It is not surprising that a very successful stage version of *The Pit* appeared in 1904. Part of the novel's dramatic effect no doubt derives from the inherent dramatic possibilities of a love triangle or a business crisis. But Norris was perhaps encouraged to think dramatically by his friendship with the Hernes. He met Katherine and Julie Herne, the widow and daughter of the playwright-actor James A. Herne, in the winter of 1901-1902, when he was writing *The Pit*. For some time he thought seriously of collaborating with them on a dramatic version of *The Octopus*,[58] and though this idea was not pursued, it seems to have sharpened

his sense of the dramatic element in fiction at the moment he
was writing *The Pit.*

6

The Pit breaks so neatly into the love triangle and the story of
Jadwin's corner that it seems almost inevitable to deal with these
plots independently before discussing the novel as a whole. Of the
two, the wheat story is the simpler and the more forceful. Curtis
Jadwin has made a fortune in real estate and seldom speculates
on the wheat exchange. He is a strong, self-controlled man, but,
like Vandover, Condy, and Magnus, he has a powerful gambling
instinct, and after some early victories at the Board of Trade he is
drawn more and more into speculation. He had always scoffed at
the possibility of cornering the market, but during the fourth
year of his marriage he discovers that he is close to a corner and
that he cannot resist proceeding. At first successful, he is overcome by a tragic hubris, a pride in his strength, which blinds him
to approaching disaster. At last his corner is broken by an influx
of large supplies of wheat, his immense holdings fall in value,
and he loses his entire fortune.

Jadwin's corner bears directly on the principal theme linking
the individual novels of the epic of the wheat. As in *The Octopus,*
the wheat fulfills its role as a benevolent world force in spite of
those who try to impede its progress. Norris' primary image of the
pit is therefore of a maelstrom, of a whirlpool whose turbulence
is caused by the flow of millions of bushels of wheat through its
narrow confines before the current widens again to reach a sea of
consumers. Jadwin attempts to thwart this flow—to corner the
supply and thereby raise the price of the wheat he owns. The
blocked demand, however, not only raises the price, but also
causes an immense increase in supply, and Jadwin is eventually

thrust aside by an avalanche of wheat. His relationship to the pit is the same as that of the railroad operators to the railroad. Like Shelgrim, he attempts to excuse his actions:

> "You think I am willfully doing this! You don't know, you haven't a guess. I corner the wheat! Great heavens, it is the wheat that has cornered me. The corner made itself. I happened to stand between two sets of circumstances, and they made me do what I've done" (IX, 270).

Like Shelgrim, Jadwin has failed to distinguish between the inevitability of a social institution—here a means of distributing wheat—and the responsibility that men have for their actions within such an institution. Jadwin's fault is that his gambling instincts and his desire for power have led him to interfere excessively with the great natural law of supply and demand which governs the production and movement of wheat. When his corner is about to collapse, he realizes for the first time that he has not been opposing other dealers;

> it was [rather] that fatal New Harvest; it was the Wheat; it was . . . the very Earth itself. What were those scattered hundreds of farmers of the Middle West, who because he had put the prices so high had planted as never before? What had they to do with it? Why, the Wheat had grown itself; demand and supply, these were the two great laws the Wheat obeyed. Almost blasphemous in his effrontery, he had tampered with these laws, and had roused a Titan. He had laid his puny human grasp upon Creation, and the very earth herself, the great mother, feeling the touch of the cobweb that the human insect had spun, had stirred at last in her sleep and sent her omnipotence moving through the grooves of the world, to find and crush the disturber of her appointed courses (IX, 357-58).

Jadwin is metaphorically buried under the wheat he thought he could control, just as S. Behrman, the self-styled "Master of the Wheat," is literally drowned by it at the close of *The Octopus.*

Norris' method in both novels was to use the wheat (usually capitalized) as a metaphor or symbol for natural law. He gained dramatic emphasis by this substitution but he sacrificed clarity. When he speaks of the Wheat as an impersonal, omnipotent force, as he does in both novels, he does not mean that no one grows it or ships it or trades it, but rather that these activities are regulated by a natural law which is impersonal and omnipotent. A man engaged in these processes has free will within the limited sense that he may choose to accept or ignore the laws governing them. Norris has been accused of stupidity and ignorance for saying "the Wheat had grown itself,"[59] but if one recognizes that he has equated the object with the economic principle regulating the production of the object, his statement is more respectable and meaningful.

Although Jadwin's role is parallel to those of Shelgrim and S. Behrman, he is very unlike them personally. He lacks both Shelgrim's intellect and Behrman's villainy. He is rather a kind of tragic hero—a man of strength and good will whose one major flaw causes him to be cast down, after a titanic struggle, by the moral forces of the universe. But though Norris succeeds in involving us in the dramatic and narrative excitement of Jadwin's corner, building up to an excellent climax on the day it breaks, he fails to convince us of Jadwin's essential worth or of the poignancy of his fall. He fails on two grounds. First, his portrait of Jadwin depends too heavily on a superficial concept of the American man of virtue. Jadwin dislikes opera and most modern novels, but admires country songs and Howells' "real-life" characters. He loves to tinker with his steam yacht or discuss his horses, he is proud of his fast trotter, and he believes in doing good by increasing the operating efficiency of Sunday schools. He is an epitome of the self-made businessman of simple tastes and strong will who has made our country great. He is Benjamin

Franklin, Leatherstocking, and Lincoln seen through the distorting prism of a commercial society.[60]

Jadwin also fails to convince as a tragic figure because of the nature of his final self-recognition. He admits to Laura that he has been to blame for their estrangement and for her lapse. But his self-blame is entirely on this personal level: he believes his speculation was harmful because of its effect on his domestic life. Although Norris commented in several places on the social effects of Jadwin's corner—thè disrupted wheat market, the starving peasants—Jadwin himself ignores this aspect of his speculation.[61] He uses his corner for a personally satisfying moral act when he rehabilitates the ruined speculator Hargis and punishes the scoundrel who had cheated Hargis, but he refuses responsibility for the broad social impact of his corner. Norris wants us to believe at the end of the novel that Jadwin has been regenerated by self-recognition and by the rebirth of love. But given the shallowness of his self-blame and the limited range of his human sympathies (no "poor naked wretches" here), we are neither moved nor convinced.

Jadwin lacks the breadth of understanding and of feeling that usually characterizes a tragic figure, and his fall also lacks the poignancy that surrounds the collapse of McTeague's world. He is simply a businessman who has taken a chance and lost. If Norris had kept the portrayal of Jadwin within these bounds, he might have been an effective source of pathos, like Magnus Derrick. Instead, he attempted to magnify Jadwin's character and struggle—for example, by using military and Napoleonic imagery to describe the corner—and Jadwin is therefore often wooden and occasionally unbelievable. Jadwin differs from Howells' Silas Lapham and Dreiser's Frank Cowperwood, two other businessman characters in American fiction of this period, in that he alone does not accept the social responsibility of his business actions. Lapham refuses to harm the public, and Cowperwood says the public be damned, but when Jadwin is told of starving Italian peasants, he cries, " 'It's a lie!' " (IX, 320). Even so, Jadwin is in one way the more significant portrait, though Norris was probably unaware of this implication of his characterization. For Jadwin's substitution of a personal philanthropy (his Sunday school work and his generosity to Hargis) for a broader social consciousness has been the generic American solution to the conflict posed by a Christian conscience and a business society.

Laura is the primary character in the love plot of *The Pit*. Like Lloyd Searight in *A Man's Woman*, she progresses from a proud self-centeredness to a selfless acceptance of her feminine role of total involvement in her husband's work. At the opening of the novel she has three suitors: Landry Court, Sheldon Corthell, and Curtis Jadwin. She encourages all of them because their attentions flatter her vanity and satisfy her deeply emotional nature. Corthell and Jadwin are the serious contenders for her love. In the novel's excellent opening chapter, set at the opera, Norris not only introduces this triangle but also broadens its thematic implications. Corthell is a man of independent wealth who has devoted his life to the art of stained glass. He is associated in Laura's mind with Art and with a high but formalized passion— in other words, with the opera itself—and he appeals to this side of her nature. Jadwin, on the other hand, is a calm and powerful man of affairs whose strength and whose involvement in the turbulence of Life attract Laura. Corthell and Jadwin thus symbolize the opposing cultural ideals of "art" and "life"—that is, they symbolize the popular myth of the artist as a detached and therefore somewhat feminine observer of experience and the businessman as a vigorous, masculine participator in the struggle for existence. This contrast, which is also present in much of Norris' literary criticism (summed up by his call for "life, not literature"), is another example of his fundamental primitivistic anti-intellectualism. His intent in the portrayal of Corthell was not to deride all art but to emphasize that art should emerge out of the artist's involvement in the vigorous, even violent, activity of modern life.[62] Norris believed that modern artists should write novels about wheat corners rather than occupy themselves with stained glass.

Laura is won by Jadwin, not because she decides that she loves him, but because of his persistence and force. Throughout the novel Norris used the kiss to symbolize the state of the Laura-Jadwin relationship. During their courtship she had been frightened and unsure of her decision, and had withheld this symbol of love. On her marriage day, she recognizes the understanding and kindness which accompany Jadwin's love, and she responds with her own love and a kiss. The first three years of their marriage are idyllic, but when Jadwin begins to speculate heavily, their estrangement is symbolized by his neglect of the ritual farewell morning kiss. Finally, when they are reunited at the end of the novel, they kiss as they depart their old home for their new lives in the West.

Laura fails in her duty toward Jadwin in two vital ways. She does not help him fight his gambling instincts (as Blix helped Condy) and, as her sister Page tells her, she divorces herself from his business life and therefore cannot help him when he needs her support and guidance. She fails as a wife despite her potential as a "man's woman" because she is still dominated by the selfishness which characterized her life before her marriage. As she and Jadwin drift farther apart, she is consumed by self-pity, boredom, and hurt pride. She resumes her friendship with Corthell and almost allows herself to be persuaded to leave her husband for him.

The last third of the novel consists of the parallel progress of Jadwin's corner and Laura's affair. On the same day that Jadwin's corner collapses, Laura surrenders to her need for love and tells Corthell that she loves him and that she will leave with him. Jadwin returns home weak and broken, and finds Laura herself broken by her surrender to her weakness. They have both succumbed to their major flaws—Jadwin to his gambling instincts, Laura to her selfish idea of love and marriage. They are reunited in mutual guilt and pain, and out of their reunion come forgiveness and love. Laura now realizes that the major conflict in her life was not between the "two Lauras" represented by Corthell and Jadwin but between selfishness and full commitment to another. She is reborn into a "third Laura" who is no other than the ideal "man's woman" of Norris' popular novels.

When Owen Wister reviewed *The Pit* early in 1903, he summarized its love plot as "Two hearts, that should beat as one, estranged by prosperity, and by adversity united in the happy and solemn end: this, stated in its simplest terms, is the theme of 'The Pit'—a theme as old as the hills, and all the better for being so."[63] Wister was both too generous and too simple. The love plot is not all the better for being hackneyed, but rather collapses under that burden and pulls down the entire novel with it. Norris is one of our first novelists to describe the peculiarly American dilemma of the "occupationless" wife—of the woman freed from all labor and prone to a neurotic ennui. But even this theme is vitiated by its envelopment in almost all the clichés of the "poor little rich girl" popular fable, from Laura's inexhaustible and overdisplayed wealth to her longing for the simple days of the past when she was poor but happy.

Yet Laura is also a more complex figure than Wister's summary suggests. Although she is cut from the same general pattern as Norris' popular heroines, he develops her more fully and with greater depth. He portrays the force of her emotional needs with considerable insight and honesty. She is not a cardboard figure like Moran, Blix, and Lloyd, all of whom are sharply transformed by love. The same emotional self-centeredness which led her to accept the man who loved her with greatest intensity later underlies her emotional (and sexual) starvation and its manifestations in her semineurotic enthusiasms and in her almost hysterical turn to Corthell. Even her final acceptance of a "third Laura" is to be an evolution rather than a sudden conversion. In all, Laura is one of Norris' fullest portraits. Yet despite her richness, we are much closer to Trina or Blix or Hilma. Perhaps the reason for this sense of distance is that we cannot separate Laura's character from the trite and predictable love story in which she appears. We recognize the effort and thought that went into her creation, but we are not really involved in her dilemma, as we are in the fate of an Anna Karenina or an Emma Bovary. Paradoxically, we are much more concerned with Jadwin, for despite the obviousness of his character, we are caught up in the excitement and suspense of his corner. If *The Pit* illustrates anything about the art of fiction, it is that a "good story" is seldom a negligible virtue—that even Ahab and Hester would interest us less where it not for the pursuit of a whale and the secret of an adultery.

Neither the business nor the love plot of *The Pit* is really successful, yet they are more successful independently than togther. For the question that has troubled almost all critics of *The Pit* is: In what way are the two plots thematically related? They are connected in other ways, of course, since the wheat pit is a kind of mistress wooing Jadwin away from his wife, and since both plots run parallel courses and reach a simultaneous climax. But there seems to be no common theme in the two, and the critic is therefore reduced to describing what Norris perhaps intended rather than what he achieved, using *The Octopus* as a key. In that novel Annixter and Vanamee learn to accept love by shedding selfishness, a change which is aided by their perception of nature's universal benevolence as symbolized in the wheat. The wheat might be expected to play a similar role in *The Pit*, dominating both the business and the love plots. In *The Octopus*, however, all the major participants in the love stories are in direct contact with the wheat—indeed, Hilma and Angèle's daughter symbolize its cycle of growth—whereas in *The Pit* Jadwin does not fully understand the wheat (as do Annixter and Vanamee) and Laura has nothing to do with it. She learns her correct role first from her sister and then by recognizing her own selfishness.

One of the major reasons for the failure of *The Pit*, therefore, is that though Norris conceived of a novel with the same theme and structure as *The Octopus*—that is, the theme of the benevolent power of nature linking a love story and a public event—he failed to infuse a nature theme into his love plot. In *The Octopus* this task was simplified by the setting. The central characters were closely involved with either growing wheat or struggling for the land. In *The Pit*, however, not only was Jadwin's speculation considerably removed from the physical reality of the wheat, but —more vitally—Laura's lack of interest in his affairs made it very difficult to introduce a nature theme into her world. Norris does make one ineffectual attempt at such a theme, when he has Corthell explain to her the universal benevolence of racial evolution. His explanation, however, is too abstract and too brief, and it is not pursued. It has no impact on her, and she fails to relate it to Jadwin's activities. One sees, finally, that Norris was faced with an almost insoluble problem in *The Pit*. Laura's selfishness in love is like Annixter's and Vanamee's, but her selfishness takes the form of lack of involvement in her husband's affairs. The wheat functions as a thematically unifying symbol in *The Octopus* because Annixter and Vanamee use it to confirm their new values, but Laura is prohibited by her selfishness from having any contact with the wheat. Her husband could just as well be speculating in stocks and bonds as far as she is concerned. The love story of *The Pit* is that of any domestic novel in which a preoccupied husband neglects his wife; unlike the love stories of *The Octopus*, it seems unrelated to the novel's epic theme of nature's power and benevolence. As a result of this flaw, the epic theme in *The Pit* lacks force, and the work as a whole seems disjointed.

The novel's symbolism is also disjointed, since its major symbols, those involving the wheat and the pit, are present only in the business plot. An entirely different group of symbols appears in the love story. Norris uses three violent and sensational symbols for the pit. It is a whirlpool, a military battleground, and an arena for the combat of enraged animals (bulls and bears). Even more than in *The Octopus*, the wheat itself is lost as a dominant symbol because of Norris' fondness for sensational images of conflict and destruction. The symbolism in the love story is more subtle. Laura's artistic tastes, her dramatic roles, and her huge prison of a house constitute a rich symbolic key to her character and to her conflicts.

As was his practice in his major novels, Norris used a circular pattern in *The Pit*, beginning and ending with the collapse of a corner and with a portrait of the Sphinx-like Board of Trade building. Within this pattern, the novel is constructed very much like *McTeague*, since it breaks sharply at the marriage of Jadwin and Laura. As in *McTeague*, the first half of the novel contains the "rising action" of courtship and marriage while concomitantly introducing the character flaws which will later cause disruption—Laura's vanity and Jadwin's interest in speculation. After a briefly summarized idyllic period following their marriage, the second half of the novel depicts Jadwin's corner and Laura's affair. The failure of the marriage in *McTeague* is climaxed by murder, and the cynical might argue that it was principally the *Saturday Evening Post* which prevented *The Pit* from ending with Jadwin's suicide and Laura's elopement. But Norris had amply foreshadowed the theme of true love gone temporarily astray, unlike the complete loss of love in *McTeague,* and the conclusion of *The Pit* is inseparable from the total effect of the novel and is not a crudely attached "happy ending."

The Pit reveals Norris' continued success in depicting large-scale public occasions. The best scenes are the opera, the marriage, and the wheat exchange on the day Jadwin's corner breaks —scenes in which Norris conveys a coherent total effect while maintaining a complex narrative and thematic movement. He suggests something of Chicago life in these and other scenes, but this is but a faint quality in *The Pit* compared to the rich genre texture of his San Francisco novels.

Although Jadwin and Laura are the novel's principal characters, some of its minor figures are more appealing. Norris used Corthell as a static representation of one aspect of Laura's character. But though Corthell is cast in a potentially villainous role, and though his artistic interests are suspect, Norris develops him with a sympathetic fullness and implies his integrity. Ultimately Corthell is a little like Presley, a man of sensibility and perception (he, too, grasps the "larger view") who lacks experience of the rough and tumble of active life. The reader comes to respect him and finally to feel that he has been rather shabbily treated by Norris. He is always the sincere and ardent suitor, yet he is again and again rebuffed just as he is about to gain the prize. Since happy endings are the order of the day, what with Page and Landry Court also happily married at the close, one feels that something should have been arranged for Corthell as well rather than once more shuffling him off to France to study stained glass. Landry and Page are simply Condy and Blix again, though somewhat more youthful and comic than the earlier pair. At this point in his career Norris was capable of a Booth Tarkington sparkle in his sentimental love comedy. Indeed, there is probably little in Tarkington to rival Landry's solemn pledge to Page that he intends to stay up all night drinking black coffee and reading *The Stones of Venice*, so intensely has she cultivated his desire for self-improvement.

But whatever the minor excellencies of *The Pit*, the novel fails to rise above the Laura-Jadwin relationship. As in his popular novels, Norris' idea of woman as self-sacrificing helpmate to a man of action weakens whatever it touches. Although this theme occurs in *Vandover*, *McTeague*, and *The Octopus*, these novels are dominated by other concerns. Norris' failure in *The Pit*, therefore, does not mean that his major work had been completed. He had written *The Octopus* after three unimportant popular novels. It indicates rather that Norris masculine-feminine ethic was an important weakness in all his work, and that it would perhaps have continued to be so. At the same time, however, his treatment of Laura suggests that he might have ultimately portrayed women as they are rather than as moral convention held they should be.

Chapter Five

CONCLUSION

Frank Norris was not a great novelist. His work lacks the breadth and depth of human understanding that we require of the greatest writers of fiction. Even his best novels are marred by melodramatic symbolism and oversimplified moral contrasts. But *Vandover, McTeague,* and *The Octopus* will continue to be read for reasons other than their importance in late-nineteenth-century literary and intellectual history. Their permanence stems from Norris' vigorous involvement in man's universal attempt to make the unpalatable palatable, from his endeavor to translate two of the cruelly pinching facts of his own day—man as an evolutionary creature in an industrial society—into equally "factual" but emotionally acceptable fictional realities. He made this attempt not by writing novels of ideas, but rather—and this is what makes his fiction live—by imaginatively infusing into the vividly concrete world of Polk Street or the San Joaquin Valley a controlling vision of man and society. His best work, whatever its flaws, has the force of a particularized world shaped by an ordered conception of that world and by a firm craftsmanship.

I think, also, that the time has come when the reaction against the more blatant manifestations of nineteenth-century optimism has abated and we can estimate somewhat more fairly what is valid and lasting in the thought of such a temperamentally affirmative mind as Norris'. Certainly, his positive view of man and society often fails to convince, primarily because he uncritically overdramatized Le Conte's evolutionary system. Yet in its larger relevance, his thinking is not very different from that of modern evolutionary humanism. Led by such men as Julian Huxley, this movement also seeks not to destroy the religious sentiment, but to find in the evolution of man rather than in divine revelation those transcendent, universal truths which should guide men— truths which differ little from the ideals of Western civilization once these ideals are divorced from the supernatural and the theological. Norris' central vision of life, therefore, is closely allied to that dynamic, organic concept of man which in the last hundred years has in almost every phase of life replaced the static and mechanical.

Norris is not a writer who impresses when excerpted, and the many passages I have quoted fail to do him justice, particularly since they have often been his most analytical or rhetorical and therefore his worst. His great strength is in the cumulative impact of character and event—in the full effect of Vandover's decline or of Trina's greed or of the mounting tension in the San Joaquin. It is Norris' keen sense of repetitive and cumulative detail which is responsible for this effect. But we have forgotten many novelists with an equally keen sense. What absorbs us in Norris is the continuing vitality of his themes and the strength of the imagination which created their total symbolic constructs.

NOTES

Except when otherwise noted, all biographical information used in this study derives from Franklin D. Walker's *Frank Norris: A Biography* (Garden City, N. Y., 1932). References to Norris' work other than his novels are to initial publication. Later republication appears in the bibliography. I have used the following abbreviations throughout the notes:

CE: The Complete Edition of Frank Norris (Garden City, N. Y., 1928).

FWC: The Franklin Walker Collection, Bancroft Library, University of California, Berkeley.

FNC: The Frank Norris Collection, Bancroft Library, University of California, Berkeley.

Letters: The Letters of Frank Norris, ed. Franklin Walker (San Francisco, 1956).

Lundy: Robert D. Lundy, "The Making of *McTeague* and *The Octopus*" (Ph. D. diss., Univ. of California, 1956).

1. Introduction

1. Some works which I have found useful for the study of this dilemma are: John C. Greene, "Biology and Social Theory in the Nineteenth Century: Auguste Comte and Herbert Spencer," in *Critical Problems in the History of Science,* ed. Marshall Clagett (Madison, Wisc., 1959), pp. 419-46; Richard Hofstadter, "The Vogue of Spencer," *Social Darwinism in American Thought, 1860-1915* (Philadelphia, 1945), pp. 18-36; William H. Hudson, *An Intro-*

duction to the Philosophy of Herbert Spencer (New York, 1894); Morse Peckham, "Darwinism and Darwinisticism," *Victorian Studies*, III (Sept., 1959), 19-40; Robert Scoon, "The Rise and Impact of Evolutionary Ideas," and Stow Persons, "Evolution and Theology in America," in *Evolutionary Thought in America*, ed. Stow Persons (New Haven, 1950), pp. 4-42 and 422-53; John Herman Randall, Jr., "The Changing Impact of Darwin on Philosophy," *Journal of the History of Ideas*, XXII (Oct.-Dec., 1961), 435-62; and Herbert W. Schneider, A *History of American Philosophy* (New York, 1946), pp. 321-80.

2. John Fiske, *The Idea of God as Affected by Modern Knowledge* (Boston, 1885), p. xi.

3. Ibid., p. 163.

4. John Fiske, *The Destiny of Man* (Boston, 1884), p. 103.

5. John Fiske, *The Idea of God*, p. 163.

6. John Fiske, *Through Nature to God* (Boston, 1899), p. 130.

7. For an account of this transcendental background, see Persons, "Evolution and Theology in America," pp. 439-40, and H. Burnell Pannill, *The Religious Faith of John Fiske* (Durham, N. C., 1957), pp. 43-53.

8. Henry Drummond, *Natural Law in the Spiritual World* (New York, 1885), p. xxiii.

9. William H. Carruth, "Each in His Own Tongue," *New England Magazine*, N.S. XIII (Nov., 1895), 322.

10. Franklin Walker, "Frank Norris at the University of California," *University of California Chronicle*, XXXIII (July, 1931), 325.

11. Quoted by Walker, ibid.

12. *Blue and Gold* (University of California Year Book), XVIII (San Francisco, 1891), 69.

13. *Blue and Gold*, XX (San Francisco, 1893), 102.

14. Frank Todd, in an interview with Franklin Walker, April 2, 1930 (FWC).

15. See Bernard Moses, "Social Science and Its Method," *Berkeley Journal of Social Science*, I (Jan., 1880), 1-14.

16. There is no description of this course in the 1893-94 catalogue (Norris took it in the fall of 1893), but it is described in the

Register of the University of California, 1892-93, p. 51. For Charles Mills Gayley's evolutionary ideas, see his "A Society of Comparative Literature," *Dial*, XVII (Aug. 1, 1894), 57 and Benjamin P. Kurtz, *Charles Mills Gayley* (Berkeley, 1943), p. 119.

17. Norris' University of California transcript, Registrar's Office, Berkeley.

18. Such classmates of Norris' as H. W. Rhodes and Seymour Waterhouse recalled, in interviews with Franklin Walker on April 20 and June 5, 1930, that Norris showed much interest in Le Conte's courses. Both Charles G. Norris and Jeannette Preston (Norris' brother and widow) told Walker (on May 16 and May 8, 1930) that Norris remembered and spoke highly of Le Conte (FWC).

19. Joseph Le Conte, "Evolution and Human Progress," *Open Court*, V (April 23, 1891), 2779.

20. There were approximately 100 students in each of these courses the year Norris took them (course reports in the Registrar's Office, Berkeley). For Le Conte as a lecturer, see Josiah Royce, "Joseph Le Conte," *International Monthly*, IV (Sept., 1901), 324-34.

21. *Blue and Gold*, XVIII (San Francisco, 1891), 113.

22. *The Autobiography of Joseph Le Conte*, ed. William Dallam Armes (New York, 1903), pp. 257, 336.

23. There has been little study of Le Conte's position in the history of American evolutionary theism, since consideration of him is usually overshadowed by that given Fiske. But see Eugene W. Hilgard, "Biographical Memoir of Joseph Le Conte," in *Biographical Memoirs of the National Academy of Sciences*, VI (1909), 147-218 and Persons, "Evolution and Theology in America," pp. 441-47.

24. Quoted from Joseph Le Conte's comments on Josiah Royce's *The Conception of God: An Address Before the Union* (Berkeley, 1895), p. 49. Le Conte in this brief reply to Royce's address sums up his basic ideas.

25. Joseph Le Conte, *Evolution: Its Nature, Its Evidences, and Its Relation to Religious Thought* (2nd ed., rev.; New York, 1891), p. 353.

26. Ibid., p. 356.

27. Ibid., p. 96.

28. Le Conte, "Evolution and Human Progress," p. 2780.
29. Le Conte, *Evolution*, p. 329.
30. Ibid., p. 330.
31. Ibid., p. 375.
32. Although Franklin Walker pointed out in 1932 the possible influence of Le Conte on Norris, Robert D. Lundy has been the only critic to pursue this lead. Lundy, however, confines his study primarily to Le Conte's influence on the optimistic conclusion of *The Octopus*. See Lundy, pp. 272 ff.
33. Gelett Burgess, in a letter to Franklin Walker, Oct. 18, 1930 (FWC).
34. William Dean Howells, "Frank Norris," *North American Review*, CLXXV (Dec., 1902), 772.
35. Norris, "A Plea for Romantic Fiction," *Boston Evening Transcript*, Dec. 18, 1901, p. 14.
36. These characteristics appear in Vandover and in Condy Rivers, Norris' most autobiographical figures. When Walker interviewed Norris' University of California classmates in 1930, several recalled his predilections in this direction, though more as common attributes of fraternity life than as excessive vices. See Walker's interviews with Ralph Hathorn, April 15, 1930; H. W. Rhodes, April 20, 1930; and Harry M. Wright, April 7, 1930; and George Gibbs' letter to Walker, June 10, 1930 (FWC).
37. Norris, "Ethics of the Freshman Rush," *Wave*, XVI (Sept. 4, 1897), 2.
38. *Overland Monthly*, Ser. 2, XXI (1893), 244.
39. Ibid., p. 251.
40. Ibid., pp. 258-59.
41. Ibid., pp. 259-60.
42. *Overland Monthly*, Ser. 2, XIX (1892), 347.
43. *Pilgrim*, VI (1902), 33.

2. *Vandover and the Brute* AND *McTeague*

1. See Barrett Wendell, "English at Harvard," *Dial*, XVI (Mar. 1, 1894), 131-33, and Charles Mills Gayley, "English in the University of California," *Dial*, XVII (July 16, 1894), 29-32.

2. Norris' application, Registrar's Office, Harvard University.

3. See *Blix*, CE, III, 10.

4. It is difficult to determine when Norris began reading Zola. Most of his Berkeley classmates recalled his enthusiasm for Zola, but some date it as early as his sophomore year while others believe that it derived from a course in realistic French literature which he took as a senior (FWC). His junior year is the most probable period of his discovery of Zola.

5. Norris' only explicit mention of it is in his review of Zola's *Rome* in the *Wave*, XV (June 6, 1896), 8, when he referred to Zola's theme of hereditary determinism in that novel.

6. Norris, "Zola as a Romantic Writer," *Wave*, XV (June 27, 1896), 3.

7. He particularly admired Zola's nondidactic method and his ability with large canvases. See his review "Zola's *Rome*," *Wave*, XV (June 6, 1896), 8 and "Frank Norris' Weekly Letter," *Chicago American Literary Review*, July 13, 1901, p. 8.

8. Emile Zola, *L'Oeuvre*, trans. Thomas Walton as *The Masterpiece* (London, 1950), p. 162.

9. Emile Zola, *Thérèse Raquin*, trans. Philip G. Downs (London, 1955), p. viii. Zola used as an epigraph for this novel Taine's famous remark that "vice and virtue are products just as are vitriol and sugar."

10. Norris to Charles F. Lummis, April 9, 1900; published by Donald Pizer, "Ten Letters by Frank Norris," *Quarterly News-Letter* of the Book Club of California, XXVII (Summer, 1962), 56.

11. Lundy, pp. 104-105, has determined this chronology by an examination of the extant themes (in the FNC) which Norris wrote for Gates' composition class.

12. The account of English 22 which follows is derived from Lundy, pp. 42-53; *Annual Report of the President and Treasurer of Harvard College, 1894-95* (Cambridge, 1896); *Harvard University: Announcement of the Department of English, 1894-95* (in the Harvard archives); and Robert Morss Lovett, *All Our Years* (New York, 1948), p. 45. It is interesting to note that E. A. Robinson took courses from Gates in 1891-92 and liked him as a teacher.

13. *Harvard University: Announcement of the Department of English, 1894-95*, p. 13.

14. Norris to Lewis E. Gates, Feb. 22, 1899, *Letters*, p. 27.
15. Ibid.
16. My interpretation of Gates' influence on Norris differs from that of John S. Coolidge, "Lewis E. Gates: The Permutations of Romanticism in America," *New England Quarterly*, XXX (Mar., 1957), 23-38.
17. Norris, "The 'English Courses' of the University of California," *Wave*, XV (Nov. 28, 1896), 3.
18. Lewis E. Gates, *Studies and Appreciations* (New York, 1900), p. 41.
19. Ibid., p. 59.
20. See Hamilton V. Bail, "Harvard Fiction . . . ," *Proceedings of the American Antiquarian Society*, LXVIII (1958), 256, 272-73.
21. Norris, "The 'English Courses' of the University of California," p. 3.
22. FNC.
23. Charles G. Norris, *Frank Norris: 1870-1902* (New York, [1914]), p. 18.
24. Norris used *Vandover* for three other *Wave* pieces: "Western City Types: The 'Fast Girl'," XV (May 9, 1896), 5, is a portrait of Ida Wade loosely adapted from the novel; "Suggestions. II. A Hotel Bedroom," XVI (March 13, 1897), 7, is from the opening of chapter XVI; and "At Home from Eight to Twelve," XVII (Jan. 1, 1898), 7, is an almost literal use of Henrietta's dance party.
25. In late 1899, when the novel was in the hands of Grant Richards, Norris' English publisher, Norris wrote Richards, "I am afraid it is hardly available for any publisher just yet." Norris to Richards, Nov. 27, 1899, *Letters*, p. 49. Walker derived his account of Doubleday and McClure shipping the novel off to Heinemann from John S. Phillips, a Doubleday partner, but it is possible that Phillips, some thirty years after the event, confused Heinemann with Richards.
26. It appears in modified form in chapter I of *The Pit*.
27. Charles G. Norris, in an interview with Franklin Walker, June 9, 1930 (FWC).
28. Denison Cliff, "The Artist in Frank Norris," *Pacific Monthly*, XVII (March, 1907), 321.

29. Charles G. Norris, in interviews with Walker, May 16, June 9, and July 8, 1930, and in a letter to Walker, Jan. 19, 1931 (FWC).

30. Charles G. Norris, *Frank Norris*, p. 18.

31. Charles G. Norris, letter to Franklin Walker, Jan. 19, 1931 (FWC).

32. Charles G. Norris, *Frank Norris*, p. 18.

33. See note 36, chapter I.

34. See also *CE*, V, 104, 157, 181, 188, 244.

35. See ibid., pp. 82, 175, 220.

36. The only overt medical diagnosis in the novel is made by a hotel doctor who briefly examines Vandover during an attack of lycanthropy. His diagnosis is therefore of that symptom rather than of the inclusive disease.

37. For an account of the history of general paralysis, see Gregory Zilboorg, *A History of Medical Psychology* (New York, 1941), pp. 526-51.

38. The standard medical text was William J. Mickle, *General Paralysis of the Insane*, 2nd ed. (London, 1886). Mickle also wrote the account of general paralysis in the widely known and used *Dictionary of Psychological Medicine*, ed. D. Hack Tuke (Philadelphia, 1892), I, 519-44. Most contemporary studies of insanity included descriptions of general paralysis which differed little from Mickle's account.

39. Mickle, in *General Paralysis of the Insane*, p. 89, noted that early in the disease "there is a failure of capability in accurately playing musical instruments, in painting, in drawing" because "the movements of the hands become lessened in adroitness, in exactitude."

40. Lycanthropy, then as now, was usually discussed as a folk belief rather than as a mental disease. When analyzed as a mental disease, however, it was often noted, as in John C. Bucknill and D. Hack Tuke, *A Manual of Psychological Medicine* (Philadelphia, 1874), p. 211, that the disease is "intimately associated with a depressed state of the feelings—with Melancholia."

41. For Lawlor, besides Walker's account in his *Frank Norris*, see William B. Atkinson, *A Biographical Dictionary of Contempo-*

rary American Physicians and Surgeons (Philadelphia, 1880) and the *San Francisco Chronicle*, July 5, 1902, p. 1.

42. The murder was fully reported in the San Francisco newspapers on October 10, 1893, and for several days thereafter. This source was first noted by Charles Kaplan in his "Frank Norris and the Craft of Fiction" (Ph. D. diss., Northwestern Univ., 1952).

43. Eleanor Davenport, in a letter to Franklin Walker, Oct. 5, 1930 (FWC).

44. Trina's appointments are at 2:00 P.M., Tuesday, Thursday, and Saturday; English 22 met at 1:30 P.M. on those days.

45. *San Francisco Examiner*, Oct. 10, 1893, p. 12.

46. Ibid.

47. *San Francisco Examiner*, Oct. 11, 1893, p. 4 and *San Francisco Chronicle*, Oct. 12, 1893, p. 4. Collins was eventually found guilty of murder and was executed.

48. Norris, "Zola as a Romantic Writer," *Wave*, XV (June 27, 1896), 3.

49. FNC. I am indebted to Professor James D. Hart for permission to publish this theme prior to his forthcoming edition of Norris' Harvard themes.

50. Willard E. Martin, Jr., "Frank Norris's Reading at Harvard College," *American Literature*, VII (May, 1935), 203-204 and Charles Kaplan, "Fact Into Fiction in *McTeague*," *Harvard Library Bulletin*, VIII (Autumn, 1954), 381-85.

51. See, for example, Norris to Charles F. Lummis, April 9, 1900; published by Donald Pizer, "Ten Letters by Frank Norris," p. 56.

52. Norris, "Suggestions. IV. The Dental Parlors," XVI (March 13, 1897), 7; "Judy's Service of Gold Plate," XVI (Oct. 16, 1897), 6; and "Fantaisie Printaniere," XVI (Nov. 6, 1897), 7.

53. About seventy manuscript pages have been recovered (from what was a manuscript of over 300 pages) and are now in the FNC.

54. John S. Phillips, in a letter to Franklin Walker, April 18, 1932 (FWC).

55. Zola's influence on Norris is one of the most thoroughly investigated fields in Norris criticism. The two standard studies are Marius Biencourt, *Une Influence du naturalisme français en Amérique: Frank Norris* (Paris, 1933) and Lars Åhnebrink, *The Begin-*

nings of Naturalism in American Fiction (Cambridge, Mass., 1950). I rely on these two studies throughout, but will not cite them hereafter.

56. The fullest study of Lombroso's influence on Zola's conception of Jacques is by Martin Kanes, *Zola's "La Bête humaine": A Study in Literary Creation* (Berkeley and Los Angeles, 1962), pp. 35-36, 60-61. Lombroso himself critically examined Zola's dramatizations of his theories in "Illustrative Studies in Criminal Anthropology. I. 'La Bête Humaine' and Criminal Anthropology," *Monist*, I (Jan., 1891), 177-85.

57. Lombroso's major work, *L'Uomo delinquente* (Milan, 1876; 5th rev. ed., 1896) was translated as *L'Homme criminel* (Paris, 1887). An English version, adapted by Gina Lombroso-Ferrero, did not appear until the publication of *Criminal Man, According to the Classification of Cesare Lombroso* (New York and London, 1911). Lombroso's ideas, however, were well known in England and America by the late 1880's. Havelock Ellis' *The Criminal* (London, 1892) and Arthur MacDonald's *Criminology* (New York, 1893) were heavily Lombrosian, and Lombroso's translated articles appeared in such journals as the *Forum, Century,* and *Contemporary Review*. See also Arthur E. Fink, *Causes of Crime: Biological Theories in the United States, 1800-1915* (Philadelphia, 1938), pp. 99-150.

58. Kanes, *Zola's "La Bête humaine,"* p. 61.

59. Lombroso-Ferrero, *Criminal Man*, p. 24.

60. See Grant C. Knight, *The Critical Period in American Literature* (Chapel Hill, N. C., 1951), pp. 70-76.

61. Max Nordau, *Degeneration* (New York, 1895), p. 556.

62. FNC.

63. See the *Biennial Report of the State Board of Prison Directors of the State of California* for the years 1895-1898.

64. The second article was "A 'Lag's' Release," XVI (Mar. 27, 1897), 4.

65. See also Kenneth Lamott *Chronicles of San Quentin: The Biography of a Prison* (New York, 1961), p. 129.

66. *Wave*, XV, 7.

67. *Wave*, XVI, 9.

68. Eugene S. Talbot, in *Degeneracy: Its Causes, Signs, and Re-*

sults (London and New York, 1899), p. vii, noted that the topic of degeneracy received its "popular apotheosis under Lombroso and Nordau."

69. Many of Norris' characters have prominent jaws and yet are not criminals. Norris used prognathism as a crude symbol of the primitive strength which breaks down all barriers in its drive toward a goal or possession. He distinguished between criminal and non-criminal primitivism in terms of ends, not means. A prognathous Ward Bennett, for example, uses his strength beneficially, according to Norris, when he drives his men across the ice to safety in *A Man's Woman*, even though he commits inhuman acts in achieving that goal.

70. Norris also indicated on pp. 26, 155, and 362 (in almost the exact words) the unusual volatility of McTeague's animal nature.

71. Norris, "Little Dramas of the Curbstone," *Wave*, XVI (June 26, 1897), 9, and "A Case for Lombroso," *Wave*, XVI (Sept. 11, 1897), 6.

72. Although Norris' racialism appears in one form or another in all his novels, it is never a major theme. His concept of the Anglo-Saxon, however, is important for his critical ideas, and I discuss it in that context in my *The Literary Criticism of Frank Norris* (Austin, 1964), pp. 99-103.

73. William B. Dillingham, "The Old Folks of *McTeague*," *Nineteenth-Century Fiction*, XVI (Sept., 1961), 169-73.

74. The best analysis of its flaws is by Lundy, pp. 178-88.

75. Norris, "Sailing of the *Excelsior*," *Wave*, XVI, 7.

76. Norris, in a letter to W. D. Howells, Dec. 31, 1898, *Letters*, p. 23.

77. W. D. Howells, "Frank Norris," *North American Review*, CLXXV (Dec., 1902), 773.

78. Norris, "A Plea for Romantic Fiction," *Boston Evening Transcript*, Dec. 18, 1901, p. 14.

3. *Moran of the Lady Letty, Blix,* AND *A Man's Woman*

1. *Wave*, IX, 3.

2. "A Question of Ideals," *Wave*, XV (Dec. 26, 1896), 7. The

"girl of the broad chin" is the American girl as portrayed by Albert Wenzell, whose drawings Norris was comparing with Gibson's in this review.

3. "The Country Club at Del Monte," XIV (Aug. 31, 1895), 7. This anonymous article is not credited to Norris by his bibliographers, Lohf and Sheehy, but is undoubtedly by him.

4. See Jerome H. Buckley, *William Ernest Henley: A Study in the "Counter-Decadence" of the 'Nineties* (Princeton, 1945).

5. See Gelett Burgess, *Bayside Bohemia: Fin de Siècle San Francisco and Its Little Magazines* (San Francisco, 1954).

6. *Wave*, XVI, 7.

7. Eleanor Davenport, "Some Younger California Writers," *University of California Magazine*, III (Nov., 1897), 281. Mrs. Davenport, who was a friend of Norris', reported optimistically that a collection with this title was "in press."

8. *Blix, CE*, III, 114. The anonymous article on the station was "Life-Line and Surf-Boat," *Wave*, XVI (Sept. 18, 1897), 9.

9. He missed the issue of March 5, 1898; an editorial note explained that his move to New York had delayed receipt of the chapter for that week.

10. "How do you like *Moran*? I am in two minds about her end and do not now know whether she should be killed or go to Cuba with Wilbur." Norris to Eleanor Davenport, March 12, 1898, *Letters*, p. 6.

11. Norris' anti-intellectualism is the principal subject of William B. Dillingham's "Themes and Literary Techniques in the Fiction of Frank Norris" (Ph. D. diss., Univ. of Pennsylvania, 1961). I also deal with it extensively in my *The Literary Criticism of Frank Norris* (Austin, 1964).

12. See Norris to Harry M. Wright, March 13, 1898, *Letters*, p. 7.

13. Jeannette Preston recalled, in interviews with Franklin Walker on May 14 and 22, 1930, that *Blix* was partly written in the summer of 1898 and that it was completed during the winter of 1898-99 (FWC).

14. See particularly Stanley Cooperman, "Frank Norris and the Werewolf of Guilt," *Modern Language Quarterly*, XX (Sept., 1959), 252-58.

15. This same cast of mind pervades Norris' "The Opinions of

Leander," *Wave*, XVI (July 17-Aug. 21, 1897), in which he attacked drinking, smoking, and necking by San Francisco girls of good family but had no objection to these practices by "fast" girls.

16. Norris' sources for his Arctic material in *A Man's Woman* have been studied by Charles Kaplan, "Frank Norris and the Craft of Fiction" (Ph. D. diss., Northwestern Univ., 1952) and John C. Sherwood, "Norris and the *Jeannette*," *Philological Quarterly*, XXXVI (Apr., 1958), 245-52.

17. Norris, "The Evolution of a Nurse," XV (Oct. 17, 1896), 8.

18. "To my wife Jeannette, who gave me the idea of this story. Feb. 1900," *Letters*, p. 55. Jeannette remembered that she and Frank had talked over the novel in the summer of 1898; Jeannette Preston, in an interview with Franklin Walker, May 14, 1930 (FWC).

19. Norris to Isaac Marcosson, Nov., 1899, *Letters*, p. 48.

4. *The Octopus* AND *The Pit*

1. *Letters*, p. 34. Since Norris had written to I. F. Marcosson in December, 1898, that the "novel of California must now be a novel of city life" (*Letters*, p. 23), it seems clear that the idea for the trilogy occurred to him between December, 1898, and March, 1899.

2. W. D. Howells, "A Case in Point," *Literature*, I (March 24, 1899), 242.

3. *Letters*, p. 48.

4. See my "Frank Norris' Definition of Naturalism," *Modern Fiction Studies*, VIII (Winter, 1962-63), 408-10.

5. Ernest Marchand reviews this reception in his *Frank Norris: A Study* (Stanford, 1942), pp. 201-208.

6. William Rainsford, "Frank Norris," *World's Work*, V (Apr., 1903), 3276 and Jeannette Preston, in interviews with Franklin Walker, May 14 and 16, 1930 (FWC).

7. See William Rainsford's *The Reasonableness of Faith and Other Addresses* (New York, 1902) and *The Story of a Varied Life, An Autobiography* (Garden City, N. Y., 1922).

8. Jeannette Preston, in an interview with Walker, May 14, 1930 (FWC).

9. Norris, "The Novel With a Purpose," *World's Work*, IV (May, 1902), 2119.

10. Norris, "From Field to Storehouse. How a Wheat Crop Is Handled in California," *Wave*, XVI (Aug. 7, 1897), 6-7.

11. There are accounts of this event and its background in most histories of California, but see particularly Wallace Smith, *Garden of the Sun: A History of the San Joaquin Valley, 1772-1939* (Los Angeles, 1939), pp. 259-90 and Oscar Lewis, *The Big Four* (New York, 1946), pp. 385-98. The best discussion of the political and social background of *The Octopus* is by Lundy, pp. 217-69.

12. Thomas R. Bacon, "The Railroad Strike in California," *Yale Review*, III (Nov., 1894), 245. Norris was in Bacon's history classes throughout his freshman and sophomore years, 1890-92.

13. *CE*, V, 22. The pervasiveness of this attitude is illustrated by the fact that the "octopus" was a common symbol of the Southern Pacific throughout the eighties and nineties. See Lewis, *The Big Four*, pp. 292-93.

14. Jeannette Preston, in an interview with Franklin Walker, May 16, 1930, recalled that Norris knew both Baker and Miss Tarbell while at *McClure's* (FWC).

15. See particularly his *"Comida*: An Experience in Famine," *Atlantic Monthly*, LXXXIII (Mar., 1899), 343-48.

16. Norris to W. D. Howells, March, 1899, *Letters*, p. 34.

17. See Joseph Dorfman, *The Economic Mind in American Civilization* (New York, 1949), III, 216-19.

18. Norris, "Life in the Mining Regions," *Everybody's Magazine*, VII (Sept., 1902), 241-48. Norris, however, found that conditions were worse in some towns than in others.

19. One of these, "I. Notes," is in the FNC. An inside page contains a list of eighteen items "not included in I and II," suggesting the existence of at least three separate notebooks of clippings, interview notes, etc.

20. Norris' notebook, "I. Notes," pp. 3-4, 17 (FNC).

21. Oscar Lewis, *Bay Window Bohemia* (Garden City, N. Y., 1956), pp. 230-31.

22. *CE*, II, 310, 313, 318.

23. See the *Delta* of May 7, 14, 21 and the *Chronicle* of May 12, 13, 14, 1880.

24. Charles S. Greene, "Rabbit Driving in the San Joaquin Valley," *Overland Monthly*, Ser. 2, XX (July, 1892), 49-58.

25. Norris, "A Strange Relief Ship," *Wave*, XVI (June 12, 1897), 7. Norris also used this incident in *Blix*, CE, III, 22.

26. See his plea to I. F. Marcosson for information, November, 1899, *Letters*, p. 47.

27. Harry M. Wright, in an interview with Franklin Walker, April 7, 1930 (FWC), and Norris to John P. Irish, May, 1899 (*Letters*, p. 36). Jeannette Preston told Walker, in an interview on May 22, 1930, that Norris spoke to several Southern Pacific officials in San Francisco (FWC).

28. See note 19 above.

29. See Smith, *Garden of the Sun*, pp. 263, 270 ff and Irving McKee, "Notable Memorials to Mussel Slough," *Pacific Historical Review*, XVII (Feb., 1948), 19-27.

30. See C. B. Glasscock, *Bandits and the Southern Pacific* (New York, 1929).

31. See Lawrence E. Harvey, "The Cycle Myth in *La Terre* of Zola," *Philological Quarterly*, XXXVIII (Jan., 1959), 89-95. Compare particularly the close of both novels.

32. Norris in a letter to his agent, Paul Revere Reynolds, December, 1900; in Frederick Lewis Allen, *Paul Revere Reynolds: A Biographical Sketch* (New York, 1944), p. 46.

33. Marius Bewley, *The Eccentric Design: Form in the Classic American Novel* (New York, 1959), p. 292.

34. Published by Lars Åhnebrink, *The Beginnings of Naturalism in American Fiction* (Cambridge, Mass., 1950), p. 466.

35. Norris' fullest expression of this view is in his "A Plea for Romantic Fiction," *Boston Evening Transcript*, Dec. 18, 1901, p. 14.

36. Presley's success with "The Toilers" is based on the sensation caused by Edwin Markham's "The Man with the Hoe," which appeared initially in the *San Francisco Examiner* in January, 1899.

37. F. W. J. Hemmings, *Emile Zola* (Oxford, 1953), p. 236 and Joseph Le Conte, *Evolution: Its Nature, Its Evidences, and Its Relation to Religious Thought* (New York, 1891), pp. 368-69.

38. This argument resembles a common defense by monopolies

of their practices (see p. 143 below), and perhaps derives as well from Norris' interview with Huntington. It also is paralleled by the mine manager's "Blame the facts instead of the Company" in *Germinal*, trans. L. W. Tancock (London, 1954), p. 214.

39. His depiction of the fight was probably influenced by the conflicting eyewitness accounts of its origin published in the newspapers (see the *Visalia Weekly Delta*, May 14 and May 21, 1880) and by Zola's depiction of a similar battle in *Germinal* (pp. 398-411) in which accident and misunderstanding precipitate bloodshed.

40. He took History 9 (Elementary Political Economy) from Professor Bernard Moses in the Spring, 1893, term. The prescribed texts for the course were Francis A. Walker, *Political Economy*, and John Stuart Mill, *Principles of Political Economy*. (Norris' University of California transcript and the course reports listing the prescribed texts are in the Registrar's Office, Berkeley.) Although Walker explicitly divorced economics from natural theology, both he and Mill discussed the law of supply and demand as an unalterable economic law. Joseph Dorfman discusses Moses' essentially conservative economic ideas in his *The Economic Mind in American Civilization*, III, 96-98.

41. Jack London, "The Octopus," *Impressions Quarterly*, II (June, 1901), 46.

42. Thomas Bacon, "The Last Book of Frank Norris," *Impressions Quarterly*, IV (March, 1903), 12.

43. Dorfman, *The Economic Mind in American Civilization*, II, 120-21.

44. See particularly Leo Marx, "Two Kingdoms of Force," *Massachusetts Review*, I (Oct., 1959), 62-95. For a conflicting view, see Walter F. Taylor, *The Economic Novel in America* (Chapel Hill, N. C., 1942), p. 325.

45. For example, see CE, I, 88-90.

46. The idea that wheat should be shipped from California to the Far East was much discussed during Norris' day. See N. P. Chipman, "Greater California and the Trade of the Orient," *Overland Monthly*, Ser. 2, XXXIV (Sept., 1899), 195-210.

47. Lois Whitney, *Primitivism and the Idea of Progress in English Popular Literature of the Eighteenth Century* (Baltimore, 1934).

48. His most important essay of this kind is "The Mechanics of Fiction," *Boston Evening Transcript*, Dec. 4, 1901, p. 22.

49. As far as I can determine, the chronology of events in chapters I-VII of Book II would date the fight at the irrigation ditch in September. But once the fight has occurred, Norris refers to it as an event in June (for example, II, 271) in order to allow time for a number of incidents between the fight and the harvest scenes at the close of the novel.

50. Norris in a letter to I. F. Marcosson, Sept. 13, 1900, *Letters*, p. 67.

51. Charles Kaplan has studied Norris' use of the Leiter corner in "Norris' Use of Sources in *The Pit*," *American Literature*, XXV (Mar., 1953), 75-84.

52. Besides using such public buildings as the Board of Trade and the Auditorium, he based Laura's house and Jadwin's mansion on actual Chicago buildings. See Charles Kaplan, "Frank Norris and the Craft of Fiction" (Ph. D. diss., Northwestern Univ., 1952).

53. Norris, "The Frontier Gone at Last," *World's Work*, III (Feb., 1902), 1730.

54. Porter noted in an undated letter to Walker that Norris "did" him twice (FWC). See also "A Stained-Glass Artist. The Old-Time Studio in Which Bruce Porter Composes Windows," *Wave*, XVI (Aug. 14, 1897), 4.

55. Kenneth S. Lynn, *The Dream of Success: A Study of the Modern American Imagination* (Boston, 1955), pp. 201-207.

56. Charles Norris blamed Henry Lanier, a partner in the Doubleday, Page firm (Charles Norris in an interview with Franklin Walker, May 16, 1930; FWC). Theodore Dreiser wrote Edward H. Smith in 1920: "Norris wrote *McTeague* and *The Octopus*. Then he fell into the hands of the noble Doubleday who converted him completely to *The Pit*, a bastard bit of romance of the best seller variety." *Letters of Theodore Dreiser*, ed. Robert H. Elias (Philadelphia, 1959), I, 329. Dreiser had little confidence in Doubleday, Page, since that firm had suppressed his *Sister Carrie*.

57. "Ten Letters by Frank Norris," ed. Donald Pizer, *Quarterly News-Letter* of the Book Club of California, XXVII (Summer, 1962), 59-60.

58. See Norris' letters to Julie Herne, Oct. 29 and Nov. 15, 1901, *Letters*, pp. 80-82.

59. See particularly Oscar Cargill, *Intellectual America* (New York, 1941), p. 101.

60. See Robert P. Falk, "From Poor Richard to the Man in the Gray Flannel Suit: A Literary Portrait of the Businessman," *California Management Review*, I (Summer, 1959), 1-14.

61. Norris' story "A Deal in Wheat," *Everybody's Magazine*, VII (Aug., 1902), 173-80 dramatizes these effects fully. In the novel they are taken up only peripherally, primarily in the character of Cressler, who points out the baneful social effects of speculation.

62. Norris' fullest expression of this idea is in his story "Dying Fires," *Smart Set*, VII (July, 1902), 95-101. This story is also useful in interpreting Presley's artistic failure in *The Octopus*.

63. Owen Wister, "The Pit—A Story of Chicago," *World's Work*, V (Feb., 1903), 3133.

SELECTED BIBLIOGRAPHY

WORKS BY FRANK NORRIS

This list contains works by Norris referred to in the text or notes. I include the principal republications of applicable items. Abbreviations used are:

CE: *Complete Edition of Frank Norris* (Garden City, N. Y., 1928).

FNW: *Frank Norris of "The Wave,"* Introduction by Oscar Lewis (San Francisco, 1931).

LCFN: *The Literary Criticism of Frank Norris,* ed. Donald Pizer (Austin, Texas, 1964).

Novels

Blix: Puritan, V (Mar.-May, 1899), VI (June-Aug., 1899); New York: Doubleday and McClure, 1899; CE, III, 1-174.

McTeague: New York: Doubleday and McClure, 1899; CE, VIII.

A Man's Woman: San Francisco Chronicle, July 23-Oct. 8, 1899 and *New York Evening Sun,* Sept. 25-Oct. 17, 1899; New York: Doubleday and McClure, 1900; CE, VI, 1-245.

Moran of the Lady Letty: Wave, XVII (Jan. 8-Apr. 9, 1898); New York: Doubleday and McClure, 1898; CE, III, 177-326.

The Octopus: New York: Doubleday, Page, 1901; CE, I-II.

The Pit: Saturday Evening Post, CLXXV (Sept. 20, 1902-Jan. 31, 1903); New York: Doubleday, Page, 1903; CE, IX.

Vandover and the Brute: Garden City, N. Y.: Doubleday, Page, 1914; CE, V.

Poetry

"Crepusculum," *Overland Monthly,* Ser. 2, XIX (Apr., 1892), 347; *Two Poems and "Kim" Reviewed,* San Francisco: Harvey Taylor, 1930.

Yvernelle: Philadelphia: Lippincott, 1892; CE, VI, 247-314.

Short Stories

"At Home from Eight to Twelve," *Wave*, XVII (Jan. 1, 1898), 7; *FNW*, pp. 128-33.

"A Caged Lion," *Argonaut*, XXXV (Aug. 20, 1894), 4; *CE*, IV, 94-103.

"A Case for Lombroso," *Wave*, XVI (Sept. 11, 1897), 6; *CE*, X, 35-42.

"A Deal in Wheat," *Everybody's Magazine*, VII (Aug., 1902), 173-80; *CE*, IV, 171-84.

"The Drowned Who Do Not Die," *Wave*, XVIII (Sept. 24, 1898), 9, 12.

"Dying Fires," *Smart Set*, VII (July, 1902), 95-101; *CE*, IV, 113-27.

"The End of the Act," *Harvard Advocate*, LIX (Apr. 3, 1895), 13-14; *Wave*, XVI (Nov. 27, 1897), 3; *CE*, X, 82-85.

"The End of the Beginning," *Wave*, XVI (Sept. 4, 1897), 5; *FNW*, pp. 43-54.

"Fantaisie Printaniere," *Wave*, XVI (Nov. 6, 1897), 7; *FNW*, pp. 62-76.

"The Finding of Lieutenant Outhwaite," *Occident*, XX (Mar. 13, 1891), 49-51.

"The Guest of Honor," *Pilgrim*, VI (July-Aug., 1902), 8, 22; 9, 32-33; *CE*, IV, 148-65.

"Le Jongleur de Taillebois," *Wave*, VII (Dec. 25, 1891), 6-9; *CE*, X, 3-20.

"Judy's Service of Gold Plate," *Wave*, XVI (Oct. 16, 1897), 6; *FNW*, pp. 55-61.

"Kirkland at Quarter," *Saturday Evening Post*, CLXXIV (Oct. 12, 1901), 4-5.

"Lauth," *Overland Monthly*, Ser. 2, XXI (Mar., 1893), 241-60; *CE*, X, 115-47.

"Little Dramas of the Curbstone," *Wave*, XVI (June 26, 1897), 9; *CE*, IV, 19-25.

"Man Proposes—No. 2," *Wave*, XV (May 30, 1896), 7; *CE*, X, 59-62.

"Man Proposes—No. 5," *Wave*, XV (July 4, 1896), 12; *CE*, X, 72-76.

"Outward and Visible Signs. V. Thoroughbred," *Overland Monthly*, Ser. 2, XXV (Feb., 1895), 196-201; *CE*, X, 198-208.

"A Reversion to Type," *Wave*, XVI (Aug. 14, 1897), 5; *CE*, IV, 43-50.

"The Son of a Sheik," *Argonaut*, XXVIII (June 1, 1891), 6; *CE*, IV, 68-74.

"Travis Hallett's Half-Back," *Overland Monthly*, Ser. 2, XXIII (Jan., 1894), 20-27; *CE*, X, 148-61.

"Unequally Yoked," *Berkeleyan Magazine*, II (Sept. 22, 1893), 44-48; *CE*, IV, 85-93 (as "Toppan").

"The Way of the World," *Wave*, IX (July 26, 1892), 3-4.

Articles and Sketches

"*Comida*: An Experience in Famine," *Atlantic Monthly*, LXXXIII (Mar., 1899), 343-48; *CE*, X, 277-88.

"The Country Club at Del Monte," *Wave*, XIV (Aug. 31, 1895), 7.

"The 'English Courses' of the University of California," *Wave*, XV (Nov. 28, 1896), 2-3; *LCFN*, pp. 6-8.

"Ethics of the Freshman Rush," *Wave*, XVI (Sept. 4, 1897), 2.

"The Evolution of a Nurse," *Wave*, XV (Oct. 17, 1896), 8.

"Frank Norris' Weekly Letter," *Chicago American Literary Review*, July 13, 1902, p. 8; *LCFN*, pp. 53-55.

"From Field to Storehouse," *Wave*, XVI (Aug. 7, 1897), 6-7.

"The Frontier Gone at Last," *World's Work*, III (Feb., 1902), 1728-31; *CE*, VII, 53-61; *LCFN*, pp. 111-17.

"A 'Lag's' Release," *Wave*, XVI (Mar. 27, 1897), 4; *CE*, X, 94-97.

"Life in the Mining Regions," *Everybody's Magazine*, VII (Sept., 1902), 241-48.

"Life-Line and Surf-Boat," *Wave*, XVI (Sept. 18, 1897), 9.

"The Mechanics of Fiction," *Boston Evening Transcript*, Dec. 4, 1901, p. 22; *CE*, VII, 113-17; *LCFN*, pp. 58-61.

"New Year's at San Quentin," *Wave*, XVI (Jan. 9, 1897), 8; *CE*, X, 89-93.

"The Novel with a 'Purpose'," *World's Work*, IV (May, 1902), 2117-19; *CE*, VII, 21-26; *LCFN*, pp. 90-93.

"An Opening for Novelists," *Wave*, XVI (May 22, 1897), 7; *LCFN*, pp. 28-30.

SELECTED BIBLIOGRAPHY

"The Opinions of Leander," *Wave*, XVI (July 17-Aug. 21, 1897); *FNW*, pp. 220-50 (all except the sketch of July 17).
"A Plea for Romantic Fiction," *Boston Evening Transcript*, Dec. 18, 1901, p. 14; *CE*, VII, 163-68; *LCFN*, pp. 75-78.
"A Question of Ideals," *Wave*, XV (Dec. 26, 1896), 7; *LCFN*, pp. 166-68.
"Sailing of the *Excelsior*," *Wave*, XVI (July 31, 1897), 7; *CE*, X, 102-107.
"A Strange Relief Ship," *Wave*, XVI (June 12, 1897), 7.
"Suggestions. II. A Hotel Bedroom. IV. The Dental Parlors," *Wave*, XVI (Mar. 13, 1897), 7; *CE*, X, 80-81 ("A Hotel Bedroom" only).
"Theory and Reality," *Wave*, XV (May 2, 1896), 8; *LCFN*, pp. 161-62.
"Western City Types. The 'Fast Girl'," *Wave*, XV (May 9, 1896), 5; *FNW*, pp. 213-16.
"Zola as a Romantic Writer," *Wave*, XV (June 27, 1896), 3; *LCFN*, pp. 73-75.
"Zola's *Rome*," *Wave*, XV (June 6, 1896), 8; *LCFN*, pp. 162-64.

PRINCIPAL WORKS ABOUT NORRIS

I omit from this list the standard surveys of American literature and fiction.
Åhnebrink, Lars, *The Beginnings of Naturalism in American Fiction* (Cambridge, Mass., 1950). This supersedes Åhnebrink's *The Influence of Emile Zola on Frank Norris* (Cambridge, Mass., 1947).
Biencourt, Marius, *Une Influence du naturalisme française en Amérique: Frank Norris* (Paris, 1933).
Bixler, Paul H., "Frank Norris's Literary Reputation," *American Literature*, VI (May, 1934), 109-21.
Cargill, Oscar, *Intellectual America: Ideas on the March* (New York, 1941), pp. 89-107.
Carter, Everett, *Howells and the Age of Realism* (Philadelphia, 1954), pp. 236-38, 246-49.
Chase, Richard, *The American Novel and Its Tradition* (Garden City, N. Y., 1957), pp. 185-204.

Cliff, Denison H., "The Artist in Frank Norris," *Pacific Monthly,* XVII (Mar., 1907), 313-22.

Collins, Carvel, Introduction to *McTeague* (New York, 1950), pp. vii-xviii (Rinehart Editions).

Cooper, Frederic T., *Some American Story Tellers* (New York, 1911), pp. 295-330.

Cooperman, Stanley, "Frank Norris and the Werewolf of Guilt," *Modern Language Quarterly,* XX (Sept., 1959), 252-58.

Cowley, Malcolm, " 'Not Men': A Natural History of American Naturalism," *Kenyon Review,* IX (Summer, 1947), 414-35.

Dillingham, William B., "Frank Norris and the Genteel Tradition," *Tennessee Studies in Literature,* V (1960), 15-24.

———, "The Old Folks of *McTeague,*" *Nineteenth-Century Fiction,* XVI (Sept., 1961), 169-73.

———, "Themes and Literary Techniques in the Fiction of Frank Norris" (Ph. D. diss., Univ. of Pennsylvania, 1961).

Dobie, Charles C., "Frank Norris, or, Up From Culture," *American Mercury,* XIII (Apr., 1928), 412-24.

Dreiser, Theodore, Introduction to *McTeague,* CE, VIII, vii-xi.

Falk, Robert P., "From Poor Richard to the Man in the Gray Flannel Suit: A Literary Portrait of the Businessman," *California Management Review,* I (Summer, 1959), 1-14.

Folsom, James K., "Social Darwinism or Social Protest? The 'Philosophy' of *The Octopus,*" *Modern Fiction Studies,* VIII (Winter, 1962-63), 393-400.

French, Warren, *Frank Norris* (New York, 1962) (Twayne United States Authors Series).

Geismar, Maxwell, *Rebels and Ancestors* (Boston, 1953), pp. 3-66.

Goldsmith, Arnold L., "The Development of Frank Norris's Philosophy," in *Studies in Honor of John Wilcox,* ed. A. Dayle Wallace and Woodburn O. Ross (Detroit, 1958), pp. 175-94.

Hicks, Granville, *The Great Tradition* (New York, 1933), pp. 168-75.

Hoffmann, Charles G., "Norris and the Responsibility of the Novelist," *South Atlantic Quarterly,* LIV (Oct., 1955), 508-15.

Howells, W. D., "Frank Norris," *North American Review,* CLXXV (Dec., 1902), 769-78.

Selected Bibliography

Kaplan, Charles, "Fact Into Fiction in *McTeague*," *Harvard Library Bulletin*, VIII (Autumn, 1954), 381-85.

——, "Frank Norris and the Craft of Fiction" (Ph. D. diss., Northwestern Univ., 1952).

——, "Norris' Use of Sources in *The Pit*," *American Literature*, XXV (Mar., 1953), 75-84.

Kazin, Alfred, *On Native Grounds* (New York, 1942), pp. 97-102.

Knight, Grant C., *The Critical Period in American Literature* (Chapel Hill, N. C., 1951), pp. 161-68.

——, *The Strenuous Age in American Literature* (Chapel Hill, N. C., 1954), passim.

Lewis, Oscar, Introduction to *Frank Norris of "The Wave"* (San Francisco, 1931), pp. 1-15.

Lohf, Kenneth A. and Sheehy, Eugene P., *Frank Norris: A Bibliography* (Los Gatos, Calif., 1959).

Lundy, Robert D., Introduction to *The Octopus* (New York, 1957), pp. v-viii (American Century Series).

——, "The Making of *McTeague* and *The Octopus*" (Ph. D. diss., Univ. of California, 1956).

Lynn, Kenneth S., Introduction to *The Octopus* (Boston, 1958), pp. v-xxv (Riverside Editions).

——, *The Dream of Success* (Boston, 1955), pp. 158-207.

Marchand, Ernest, *Frank Norris: A Study* (Stanford, 1942).

Meyer, George W., "A New Interpretation of *The Octopus*," *College English*, IV (Mar., 1943), 351-59.

Millgate, Michael, *American Social Fiction: James to Cozzens* (London, 1964), pp. 38-53.

Moseley, Walter L., "Frank Norris' *The Pit*: A Re-Evaluation" (M.A. thesis, Tulane Univ., 1962).

Norris, Charles G., Foreword to *Vandover and the Brute* (Garden City, N. Y., 1914), pp. v-ix.

——, *Frank Norris: 1870-1902* (New York, [1914]).

Pizer, Donald, "Another Look at *The Octopus*," *Nineteenth-Century Fiction*, X (Dec., 1955), 217-24.

——, "The Concept of Nature in Frank Norris' *The Octopus*," *American Quarterly*, XIV (Spring, 1962), 73-80.

——, "Evolutionary Ethical Dualism in Frank Norris' *Vandover and the Brute* and *McTeague*," PMLA, LXXVI (Dec., 1961), 552-60.

———, "Frank Norris' Definition of Naturalism," *Modern Fiction Studies*, VIII (Winter, 1962-63), 408-10.

———, ed., *The Literary Criticism of Frank Norris* (Austin, 1964).

———, "The Masculine-Feminine Ethic in Frank Norris' Popular Novels," *Texas Studies in Literature and Language*, VI (Spring, 1964), 84-91.

———, "Synthetic Criticism and Frank Norris," *American Literature*, XXXIV (Jan., 1963), 532-41.

———, "Ten Letters by Frank Norris," *Quarterly News-Letter* of the Book Club of California, XXVII (Summer, 1962), 51-60.

Reninger, H. Willard, "Norris Explains *The Octopus*: A Correlation of His Theory and Practice," *American Literature*, XII (May, 1940), 218-27.

Schneider, Robert W., "Frank Norris: The Naturalist as Victorian," *Midcontinent American Studies Journal*, III (Spring, 1962), 13-27.

Sherwood, John C., "Norris and the *Jeannette*," *Philological Quarterly*, XXXVI (Apr., 1958), 245-52.

Taylor, Walter F., *The Economic Novel in America* (Chapel Hill, N. C., 1942), pp. 282-306.

Walcutt, Charles C., *American Literary Naturalism, A Divided Stream* (Minneapolis, 1956), pp. 114-56.

———, "Frank Norris and the Search for Form," *University of Kansas City Review*, XIV (Winter, 1947), 126-36.

———, "The Naturalism of *Vandover and the Brute*," in *Forms of Modern Fiction*, ed. William Van O'Connor (Minneapolis, 1948), 254-68.

Walker, Franklin D., *Frank Norris: A Biography* (Garden City, N. Y., 1932).

———, "Frank Norris at the University of California,'" *University of California Chronicle*, XXXIII (July, 1931), 320-49.

———, ed., *The Letters of Frank Norris* (San Francisco, 1956).

Wright, Harry M., "In Memoriam—Frank Norris, 1870-1902," *University of California Chronicle*, V (Oct., 1902), 240-45.

INDEX

205